FLENTROP IN AMERICA

Plate 1. Duke University Chapel, Durham, North Carolina

FLENTROP IN AMERICA

AN ACCOUNT OF THE WORK AND INFLUENCE OF THE DUTCH ORGAN BUILDER D. A. FLENTROP IN THE UNITED STATES, 1939-1977

BY
JOHN FESPERMAN

RALEIGH:
THE SUNBURY PRESS
1982

Library of Congress Cataloging in Publication Data

Fesperman, John T.
  Flentrop in America.

  Bibliography: p.
  Includes index.
  1. Flentrop, D. A. (Dirk Andries), 1910–   .
2. Organs—Construction. I. Title.
ML424.F6F5   786.6'3'0924   82-3366
ISBN 0-915548-14-3   AACR2

First edition. This is copy number 372 of an edition of 2000.

Printed for The Sunbury in Raleigh, North Carolina, United States of America.

Voor Marian Flentrop
en haar goede zorgen.

THE PUBLICATION OF THIS BOOK
was marked by
the presentation of copy number one to
HER MAJESTY QUEEN BEATRIX
of the Netherlands

in the bicentennial year of relations
between the Netherlands and the United States
April 20, 1982
St. Columba's Church
Washington, District of Columbia

SUBSCRIBERS

SUBSCRIBERS

SUBSCRIBERS

SUBSCRIBERS

SUBSCRIBERS

CONTENTS

FOREWORD

During the early nineteen fifties, the classical revival in American organ building, unlike its couterpart in harpsichord building, was progressing at an exceedingly slow pace. Frank Hubbard and William Dowd, who were revolutionizing the harpsichord industry along classical lines, had educated themselves through the study of antique instruments; but not one organ builder in this country had decided to risk a return to tracker action. This was not altogether a matter of pride or perversity among organ builders; they were best equipped to continue in established patterns while making less costly gestures toward the classical revival growing in continental Europe. American builders and organists of that time were inclined to defend "modern convenience" and technology, rather than embarking on reforms leading them into unfamiliar territory. Instruments such as those Bach knew were still generally considered primitive.

The harpsichord, on the other hand, did not carry a burden of recent history, since it had been in "moth balls" for a hundred and fifty years. Modern builders were free to pick it up where the eighteenth century had left off. Additional impetus was given to its popularity as other period instruments were brought back for performances: recorders, baroque flutes, and early forms of stringed and reed instruments, all of which required the harpsichord for continuo realization. Thus, by the mid-fifties, only the organ among the historical instruments remained relatively untouched by the classical revival. In harpsichord building Hubbard and Dowd were assuming world leadership, but in American organ building only one voice spoke for the future, that of Charles Fisk, who alone had committed himself to tracker action as the foundation of classical organ design.

After World War II, the leadership in American organ building had been held by Holtkamp of Cleveland, and Aeolian-Skinner of Boston. Their respective chiefs, Walter Holtkamp, Sr., and G. Donald Harrison, did travel in Europe, where they acquainted themselves both with ancient organs and with developments in modern organ building, especially in England. In 1951, Holtkamp, Sr. was impressed with Andreas Silbermann's early-eighteenth-century instrument at Ebersmunster, but he was not moved to reshape his thinking according to early models. Rather, he put to practical use the latest thing in England, which he observed during the same trip: Compton's unified Cornet 32' for the Pedal. He also chanced to meet D. A. Flentrop, whose new tracker organ in Loenen-aan-de-Vecht impressed him more than any of the new tracker organs he heard in Germany or Denmark. A warm friendship developed from that encounter and contributed to the gradual rise to prominence of Flentrop's reputation in the United States.

Neither Holtkamp nor Harrison foresaw the course of events, despite two important factors. For one, the finest tracker instruments being made could be imported from Europe at substantially lower cost than the best American organs of that time, all of which had electro-pneumatic key action. During the late fifties both Flentrop and Beckerath organs with tracker action were being shipped and installed in this country at a cost of less than $1000 per stop. But more important, the leaders of the electro-pneumatic organ industry failed to appreciate the enormous influence of the Fulbright scholarship program. Dozens of young American organists and musicologists received the opportunity to study the classical revival at first hand, and to study beautiful antique instruments over an extended period of time. They were to be the professors and church musicians in the next decade who would insist that the purchase of tracker organs was a necessity for the performance of early music.

Both Holtkamp and Harrison, it is true, continued to hold sway as standard-bearers of what they termed the "American classical organ." Holtkamp had espoused the musical advantages of slider chests for some time, but built them only for the main division of his larger instruments. Both builders relied on exposed pipework and "classical" stoplists to carry the weight of their musical argument, thus ignoring numerous essential requirements for classical design.

Into the void moved Beckerath and Flentrop, the former with a magnificent four-manual tracker organ in Cleveland (1957) scarcely a mile from the Holtkamp factory. But eventually it would be Flentrop who gained the strongest support when his work was endorsed by the indefatigable E. Power Biggs. The tracker movement in the United States gained much-needed publicity and substance through Biggs's superb recordings on the Flentrop organ in the Busch-Reisinger Museum at Harvard University, which had been installed as a result of Biggs's own efforts. These recordings not only educated the American public on the subject of classical organ music, but they made Flentrop the most familiar organ builder from the Old World.

Although writing on "Flentrop in America," John Fesperman has not limited himself to Flentrop's activity in this country. This would hardly have been possible, since Flentrop's influence here was the more profound for his having been active in the restoration of early instruments in Holland and Portugal. It was perhaps this facet of his work more than any other that brought about the changes in his credo when it came to building new organs. In reviewing the facts of an international career, one cannot resist musing on the gradual modifications that can be observed in Flentrop organs sent to the United States between 1956 and 1976. It has been a mere twenty years, but so much has happened in organ building. A study of these modifications and the thinking that led Flentrop to espouse them would outline the history of the classical revival in organ building during those years.

And what if Flentrop, or Beckerath, had moved to this country in the fifties, as a consequence of the threat of Russian invasion of Western Europe during the Korean crisis? Could either of them have survived, so far removed from the organs that inspired their work most profoundly? Holtkamp's invitation to Flentrop to share space in his workshop was surely a generous one; but had Flentrop been forced to accept it, the development of new viewpoints among the European leaders in the next two decades might not have influenced his work. Thus, we can conclude that these two giants from Holland and Germany have contributed most by serving us from a distance, while we have had time to gather our forces to carry on in the direction so ably pointed out to us. We now have proof that twenty-year-old tracker organs built by Flentrop can be as good as new, while the electro-pneumatic instruments of the same time have failed. On the basis of these models of craftsmanship and their superb performance, much progress has been made in a native industry. Without such examples, Charles Fisk and his younger colleagues could not have come so soon to maturity.

—Fenner Douglass

PREFACE

This account of D. A. Flentrop's work in the United States has its origin in the 1950's, when the writer was studying and travelling in Europe, largely in the Netherlands. The bias implicit in being both an organist and an admirer of Flentrop's work is hereby acknowledged, and readers are assured of the intent, at least, to spare them a surfeit of fond recollections. The warm and lengthy friendship which made this writing possible is best summarized in a personal note:

I first met Dick Flentrop in the summer of 1951, while I was enroute to study at the Mozarteum in Salzburg. He took me first of all (in an ancient Ford) to see a new organ in the lovely old town of Loenen on the river Vecht. The pivotal importance of this instrument, especially for barnstorming American students, could hardly be appreciated at that time. Embodied for the first time in the Loenen organ were the basic principles of classic design at which Flentrop had been aiming from the start. Needless to say, no one dared imagine then that the influence of this beguiling instrument would one day be felt throughout the United States—from Salem to Harvard, Seattle, Oberlin and Duke, and more.

Returning in 1955-6 as a Fulbright Scholar in the Netherlands, much of my year was spent in the Flentrop workshops in Zaandam, combined with visits to new and restored organs throughout the country and practice on the new organ in the Kruiskerk at Amstelveen, largely through the good offices of Flentrop. Returning again in the summers of 1957, -58, and -59, there was the special excitement of making tapes of the restored Schnitger organ at Zwolle, observing construction of the instrument destined for the Busch-Reisinger Museum at Harvard, coming to know more new and old organs each time. Throughout these instructive and exhilarating times, for myself as well as for other inquiring Americans, the quiet presence of Flentrop was continually felt—not only as preceptor, but also as friendly host and guide to foreigners. So, the following account has to be written almost as much from a familial standpoint (a good Dutch tradition), as from a professional one.

—J. F.

ACKNOWLEDGMENTS

Very special gratitude must first be expressed for the use of extensive correspondence, to Margaret Power Biggs, Fenner Douglass, and Charles Fisk. For much helpful information regarding specific instruments thanks is due John Mueller, Peter Hallock and Beth Berry Barber, William Weaver, Donald Willing, Schuyler Robinson, Hans Steketee, and Cees van Oostenbrugge.

Many helpful suggestions came from Fenner Douglass, William Dowd, Charles Ferguson, Charles P. Fisher, Margaret Epes, and Barbara Owen, who reviewed the initial draft.

Appreciation is also acknowledged for time away from the Museum, granted by the Smithsonian Institution, and to Richard Parsons, for suggesting and encouraging this work.

Photographs were made or generously supplied by the following: Pl. 1, 2 — Duke University News Bureau; Pl. 3 — Wim Van Duyn; Pl. 11, 17 — Laura Mueller; Pl. 15 — Keller of Belmont; Pl. 16 — Oberlin College News Bureau; Pl. 25 — Schuyler Robinson; Pl. 41 — David Gibson. An immense debt is owed D. A. Flentrop himself for his patience and willingness to supply material for an account which he neither sought nor expected, and to Marian Flentrop both for her hospitality in Holland and her benign support in numberless ways. Quotations from Flentrop not otherwise noted are from conversations during June 1979.

LIST OF DISPOSITIONS

The dispositions begin on page 93.

FLENTROP IN AMERICA

Plate 2. Duke University Chapel, Durham, North Carolina

I. EMISSARY FROM THE NETHERLANDS: FLENTROP AND THE AMERICAN ORGANBUILDING SCENE

Flentrop States His Case: Unity and Simplicity

". . .It is extremely difficult to write about organs. Organs must be seen, played and, above all, heard. First, we must learn how to look at them and how to listen to them, so that we do not expect an organ to resemble something which it is not, or to sound like something other than an organ." This eloquent opening statement is from D. A. Flentrop's address delivered at the national convention of the American Guild of Organists in New York in the summer of 1956. It is appropriately underlined in the manuscript by his friend E. Power Biggs. Both the statement and the association are characteristic of the man and his work: Flentrop's designs, however elegant, always strive for unity and simplicity; and he has always turned an attentive ear to the counsel of the musicians who play his instruments.

From the early 1950's through his retirement on May 1, 1976 as *Directeur* of the Flentrop Orgelbouw, D. A. Flentrop's presence was felt in the furthest reaches of the American organ scene.[1] His leadership was central to the mainstream of developments during these years, as the number of his instruments built for the U.S.A. alone indicates. That his output for this country was larger than that of any of his major colleagues is striking, but there is a great deal more to the story than the numbers, or even the quality, of his instruments. He never came into a new situation as an entrepreneur, but as an advocate for the best possible solution. The inescapable result was that he was immediately dealing with people who in their wish to be instructed, found themselves becoming first of all his friends.

The organ builder and the man

Flentrop is the first to insist that "Without my staff, I would have been nothing." Nonetheless, the following account is about the organs and the attitudes which distinguish the American work of D. A. Flentrop the man, rather than the firm. It proceeds from the four-stop Positief made in 1954 for the University Presbyterian Church, San Antonio, through the monumental organ for Duke University Chapel, dedicated in 1976, and the completion in 1978 of the restoration of the great eighteenth-century organs of Mexico Cathedral.

Since the man cannot be separated from his work or his American colleagues, much of what is written here comes from information supplied by the musicians who were associated with Flentrop in the construction of some ninety-three instruments in the United States.[2] So, too, is this account inevitably a personal one, written from a musician's point of view about the work of an instrument maker. It is the recounting of the work of an exceptional human being, whose influence in this country has affected not only the writer, but scores of other musicians, teachers and organbuilders, chiefly by making them consider anew the organ as, first of all, a means for making music.

It is clear that D. A. Flentrop is not the only organbuilder of the first rank who has figured in the American scene in the third quarter of the century. His response to his colleagues, who were also competitors, has been consistently generous, and he has not hesitated to point to their achievements.[3]

He has always been keenly aware that the way a musician uses an organ can drastically affect its success. Of the early public use of a new instrument (Rotterdam Concert Hall), he observed,[4] "Marie Claire Alain played a magnificent concert in Rotterdam . . . . She liked the organ very much . . . . We organbuilders don't make the organs, the organists do (or don't, sometimes)."

Two other aspects of Flentrop's character must be acknowledged to account for his rapport with others, especially musicians, and the affection with which they almost inevitably responded. First, he grew up not only as an organbuilder, but as a player, having been organist in the Hervormde Kerk in Westzaan from 1928 to 1951, as had his father before him in the nearby Westzijder Kerk and elsewhere. He therefore was able to bring to the design of his instruments a good understanding of the problems which face the player in different sorts of repertoire. Second, for all his intensity and energy, he retained a playful sense of humor in dealing with friends and colleagues. Referring to the rainy Dutch climate and sympathizing with E. Power Biggs about Boston winter weather, he wrote (20 February 1959), "Brrr, what a climate you do have, blizzards, snowstorms, cancelled concerts and so on. Look at our beautiful weather we always (?) have."

Another quality is central to Flentrop's attitude to organbuilding, especially where artistic standards for good design came into question: a good-natured decisiveness. Typically he wrote to Fenner Douglass (21 November 1956) regarding a possible design for Fairchild Chapel at Oberlin: "An extra soft stop is not necessary, when we voice the Roerfluit and the Gedekt in the right way. The organ has the right size for the chapel. I dislike to make it larger, even if I could get twice as much money for it." And later, also to Douglass (13 November 1966) concerning thoughts for an article about organ design: "Fine organists may influence organbuilders, but the final decisions have to be made by the one who is responsible for the instrument. And who else should be responsible than the builder himself? How else can he create a piece of art? Ever heard of a painter or sculptor, who made a painting or a sculpture designed by the commissioner, or even worse, by a committee?"

Restoration and learning from the past.

In order to understand Flentrop's work in the creation of new instruments, it is vital to realize that the restoration of important old organs has been a constant priority with him from the beginning of his career. His first restorations took place in north Europe, beginning in 1934 with an organ by Barend Smit (1664)[5] in Edam and in 1936, the Christian Müller organ in Beverwijk (1756), during the time when his father was still active. Then came the large Schnitger organs at Alkmaar and Zwolle, the Moreau organ in Gouda, continuing with restorations in Lisbon, Evora and Coimbra in Portugal and later, in Mexico. The insights gained from this painstaking work were reflected in the design of new instruments.

Consistent with Flentrop's strongly-held views about the nature of the organ is a refined historical sense and a doughty respect for the work of the past. The humility with which he approaches early instruments is apparent by his description of the Schnitger organ of 1723 in the Michaelskerk at Zwolle. Speaking of the deplorable state of the instrument after it had undergone many changes in the nineteenth and twentieth centuries, he wrote:[6] "It can well be imagined that after all these alterations the organ neither sounded well nor was easy to play. The fault was not Schnitger's, but arose from the complete lack of understanding of later builders who worked on the organ."

Typically for that time, there had initially been a proposal to electrify this organ, its size being thought to preclude restoration with the original mechanical action. Flentrop's response was that the organ had originally worked well, even been praised in its own day for its light action (by Joachim Hess in 1774, in his *Dispositiën der merkwaagdigste kerkorgelen*). Why should it not work properly again, if returned to the state in which Schnitger left it? When Flentrop was asked, during the negotiations for the restoration, "Whether he could make a restoration in the old style, retaining the tracker action, he answered without hesitation, Yes."[7] He later acknowledged, "I shivered a little," recognizing the formidable challenge which this organ presented.

Commenting further about the Zwolle restoration and the lessons it taught, he wrote,[7a] "In the Zwolle organ we learned a lot about the relation between the several parts of an organ. How these parts can make a bad or a fine instrument. When we started to work at the Zwolle organ, we found that many ranks of original pipes had been replaced by other pipes of lower pitch and wider scale. This resulted in wider openings of the sliders and topboards. This extra use of air resulted in wider pallets, or of further opening of the pallets, resulting in its turn in a very heavy touch of the keys. . . . To come back to normal playing action, it was necessary to come back to the original pitch (one note sharp), to the original specification, to the original scales, and after that had been done, to the original action. . . .

"My goal to make organs with a fine, responsive action, with a clear sound, rich in overtones and with an expressive accent at the beginning of each note, was strongly supported by what I had learned from the builders of the past."

Learning "a lot about the relation between the several parts of an organ" points to the concept of unity in a design, which is the cornerstone of Flentrop's approach, about which more will be heard later. His work and influence in the United States and Europe must be seen within the context of the general principles inherent in organbuilding from the earliest days. Despite the strong personality which characterizes his own instruments, his description of the Zwolle restoration further reminds us that[6] "The aim was to do justice as completely as possible to the true worth of the Schnitger organ." Speaking of the mutilated pipework, he notes that the problem was to find "the best thing to do in order to return it to its original state" and, of the voicing of the organ, ". . . Thus, personal taste is relegated to the background, because the old, original pipes gave a clear indication of the tonal direction to be followed . . .."

The earlier restoration of the Edam (1934) and Beverwijk (1936) organs came at a time when restoring old instruments, especially ones which had been altered, was usually rejected in favor of replacement with a "modern" organ with electric action. Such an undertaking was a pioneering venture in those days. While Schweitzer had begun his campaign for the *orgelbewegung* early on (his *Deutsche und Französische Orgelbaukunst . . .* had appeared in 1927), other influential works were only beginning to appear. Hans Klotz's *Über die Orgelkunst* was published in 1934, the same year Flentrop was already exhorting Dutch organbuilders (see below), and Mahrenholz's *Die Orgelregister* and *Orgelpfeifenmensuren* appeared in 1930 and 1938 respectively. With the exception of Adlung's *Musica Mechanica Organoedi* (1723-1727), which appeared in facsimile in 1931 and Dom Bédos's *L'art du facteur d'orgues* (1766), republished in 1934, very little was available for study. Very little, that is, aside from the instruments themselves, which for an organbuilder are always the prime sources.

During Flentrop's apprentice days, he was able to meet Albert Schweitzer, who was already justly famous for his efforts to preserve historical organs. This was on the occasion of Schweitzer's giving a lecture in Zaandam and also visiting an organ made by H. W. Flentrop in 1922 for the Hervormde Kerk of Koog aan de Zaan. Young Flentrop went to seek Schweitzer the next day in Amsterdam, ". . . with the result that he was to go to work for an organbuilder in Alsace. The news from Paris that a work permit was not allowed him was a great disappointment . . .."[8] Instead he went in 1927 to work and learn in the Danish firm of Frobenius.

The critical artistic importance of Flentrop's deep interest in the work of earlier builders lies in his search for viable principles of design, which could be responsibly applied to organbuilding in the present day. As early as 1934, *Het Orgel* published a paper given by Flentrop that year for the Netherlands Organists Society, in which his then advanced views were clearly stated.[9] Among his remarks were the following fundamental observations: "Mechanical slider chests compel the organbuilder to deliver better work. The best property of the slider chest is that it is not possible to make a bad disposition or poor scaling, since these faults then appear much worse than with our modern chests. . . . If one is unable to design a good new organ, then it is better to copy one of our fine old organs, of which we have so many. This is *always better* than making a poor modern organ. If we become familiar again with the art of the fine old builders, then there is no need to copy, because we can continue building on the *principles* on which the old organs are based." [italics original]

Among his first published English articles was[10] "Thoughts on Organ Design in the Netherlands," in which he sought to make this same connection in the simplest and most direct way possible, using the Oosthuizen organ of 1521 as a prototype. Again, in the 1956 New York lecture he emphasizes this attitude: ". . . This 'making again' depends entirely on a renewed understanding and appreciation of the principles which were essential for the building of good organs in former times, as well as in the present day. The principles have not changed, although we may have forgotten them from time to time during three hundred years . . . ..For me, the title "Baroque organ" is an incorrect one for the modern organ based on these principles, because it might imply either that we are using out-of-date ideas or that we merely imitate the work of earlier builders. We make a creative use of the timeless principles in terms of the musical needs of our own day . . . ."

In describing the basic components of organ design, wind supply, windchests, key and stop actions, case, disposition, placement, scaling and voicing, he begins by noting that ". . . A work of art is not created by taking only some of the necessary components, or by throwing in all the components without the most delicate distribution of emphasis among them." And speaking of locating the keyboards elsewhere than in the center of the case, he observes, "Our question is not, 'Is this possible?', which it is, but: 'Is it logical?' "

In addition to the relentless search for simple solutions to tonal and technical problems, and the quality of decisiveness combined with respect for judgements of musicians, another current runs throughout the Flentrop work. That is, the ability to learn, not only from the past and from the work of other builders, but also from one's own earlier attempts. This entails a wise regard for the unpredictability, even the mystery attendant upon the success or lack of it in a given instrument. Two conventional examples of this come to mind, one having to do with a recalcitrant wind supply, requiring much experimenting to make it function well, and the other, a key action which turned out to possess uncanny lightness and sensitivity. On asking Flentrop in both instances how these were achieved, his answer went roughly as follows: "I still am not quite sure. We tried various solutions in combination until we got the result we sought. Just what finally turned the trick we do not precisely know."

"There are no secrets in organ building," he once remarked, when asked whether his workshops were open to other builders seeking technical information. "The only secret is putting everything together in the correct way."

Teaching others.

Willingness to learn from past and present requires both the humility to recognize a superior solution and the resoluteness to persevere in artistic conventions, even in the face of adamant opposition. It also entails an openness to criticism, and, especially notable with Flentrop, not only a desire to share insights and information, but also a truly evangelical passion to *teach* others. A combination of modesty, firmness and educational zeal is everywhere evident in his dealing with musicians, students and teachers. Nowhere in his correspondence are there attempts simply to merchandise instruments, but always a patient campaign to convince the respondent of the best possible solution, with clear indications of the point at which further compromise would destroy the integrity of the design.

Workmanship and materials

A good organbuilder is first of all a good craftsman, even before he is a designer, engineer or musician. Throughout Flentrop's work, the careful attention to detail and the insistence on the best of materials has been uncompromising. "Zinc is all right for the roof of your house, but it's not good enough for organ pipes," he once remarked to the writer. "We do prefer solid wood instead of plywood, but hesitate often because of heating, air-conditioning, climate" he wrote to Fenner Douglass (13 June 1969), discussing the new organ for Florida Presbyterian College. Apropos of earlier design discussions, he added ". . . do not consider them 'the' answers but just as a consideration of former discussions . . .. We are very concerned about things like this, but often find it very difficult to find out how we want to have it and after we know that, how to accomplish it." And, in preliminary planning for the Oberlin organ, "I kept the specification in the contract as plain as possible to avoid coming into a situation where the contract wouldn't permit me to do the right thing." (6 December 1970). And earlier, (27 January 1958), about woods: "The mahogany I use is a kind of wood I know how to do with, and you have to learn that for every kind of wood . . .. I am not so eager to use wood I don't know too well, even when it is a very fine kind of wood." Even when the effect on the total design was minimal or conjectural, the quality of the materials was held paramount.

Integrity in design

Flentrop summarized his thoughts about materials and the importance of unity in design in his paper read to the American Institute of Organbuilders in October, 1978: "Like wind stability, which might be too perfect, there is another thing which leads to a kind of perfection we do not want to have any more. I mean the excessive use of pre-fabricated parts.

"It has become rather simple to put a tracker action organ together with the use of these parts. They are available everywhere and enable many people to make an action or a windchest working quite satisfactorily. They enable us to make windchests absolutely airtight and giving sufficient wind to the pipes. They enable us to install wind conductors in a couple of hours. They enable us to make so-called organ cases of plywood, mounted on a steel frame made of prefabricated parts.

"Do they make a true organ, an organ like the organ movement is directing us to? Doesn't it come dangerously close to the kind of technology of electronic — let me call them — electronic sound machines? Isn't there the danger that the so-called perfectness of these parts spoils the excellence of the organ?

"It may be argued that technology helps to make the organ durable, or that it is more economical to make such an organ, or that it enables us to make organs with less skilled people.

"This may all be very true, but have you ever heard of using these arguments in discussing the construction and qualities of violins?"

Speaking about the organbuilder's responsibility for the design again, he continued, "Going the whole way means among other things you cannot make an organ where the architect tries to dictate or influence the design of the case. Every time you try to satisfy an architect you come to results you did not want, to results which may even affect the acoustics of the building in the wrong way. Architects may be fine architects, but that does not mean they know everything."

These strong remarks about those who would meddle with his completed work characterize a temperament which is capable of indignation, albeit righteous. Flentrop's reaction to such interference with the design for Cleveland Cathedral (see Plate 30) was that of anger, a passion to which , fortunately, he was also susceptible. Nothing could be further from reality than to imply that this very human personality, this man of flesh and very Dutch blood, was unaware of the competitive energy required to reach agreement that he was the right builder for a given instrument. This was not an easy career which he made for himself, and there were struggles and disappointments, resulting in lost or thwarted opportunities. Along with battles won, there were also defeats in both Europe and the United States. Some examples are the loss of some important restoration contracts to foreign builders, the frustration attending the Carnegie Hall organ (see page 53) and the rejection of his design for the North Carolina School of the Arts in Winston-Salem, for which he had spent many hours seeking a "proper solution for a design, growing larger and larger in a space too limited for it."[11] (This commission went to Charles Fisk.) What bothered him most was not losing the contract, but not being able to see his design realized. All these were occasions for acute disappointment and frustration.

Nor did Flentrop ever discount the responsibility of being *Directeur* of a firm whose employees were dependent on his business decisions, as well as his artistic decisions, for their livelihood. There were, after all, draftsmen, voicers, pipemakers and woodworkers, always waiting for technical and artistic direction and, furthermore, these craftsmen had to be paid at the ever-rising Dutch inflation rate.

For the most part, as Flentrop himself observes, there were fewer problems with design for the United States than in Europe: "It is difficult to find a situation in the U. S. A. which was hard to solve. The reason could be that most customers were willing to accept my view on the situation, my plans. And if they didn't, the result was: No contract signed, this being refused by them or by me.

"Another reason is that every organ for the States was put up in our workshop before shipping. If there were problems, we had them in the workshop, not in the church or auditorium. When I foresaw acoustical or voicing problems, I had in several cases first a small organ, positief or 'Kistorgel' to check the acoustics. Examples: Busch-Reisinger, Oberlin, the Episcopal Church in Palo Alto (all concrete buildings), Duke University, and the Arts Center in Ottawa. Sometimes I had provided for stops or single pipes in different scales, to try out which was best

Plate 3. All Saints' Church, Palo Alto, California

Plate 4. Flentrop inspecting organ in Centre National des Arts, Ottowa

Plate 5. First Congregational Church, Branford, Connecticut

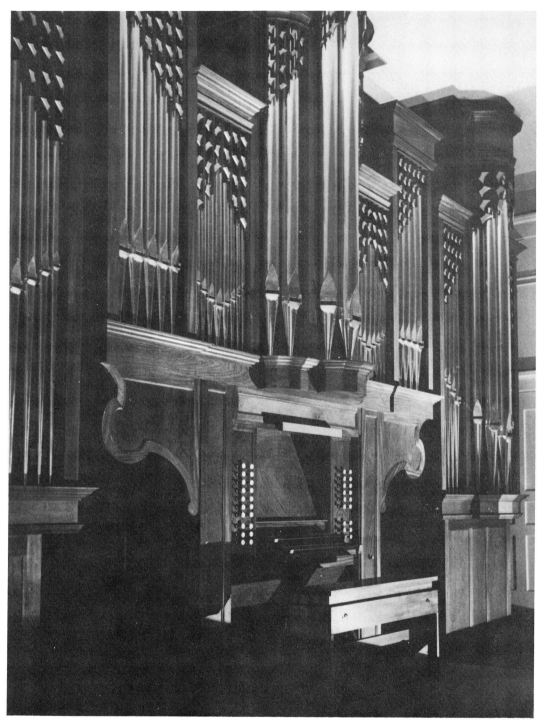

Plate 6. First Congregational Church, Branford, detail of organ

for the given situation. With this small experimental organ, we decided how to make the definite or large organ, in which way we excluded many problems."[12]

On one occasion there was discussion about the best place for the keyboards. This was in connection with the organ for Branford, Connecticut, after it had arrived at the church and was being installed: "It took some energy to convince the music committee to keep the keyboards where they belong," Flentrop recalls, noting that "the organist came in astonishment to me, asking why I installed the keyboards in the wrong direction. She meant to say that she didn't want to have the keyboards in the main case, but wanted a detached console."[13]

Flentrop's concern for live acoustics was severely tried in the Branford design: "I don't remember that I ever made an organ in a church with such poor acoustics. . . . I still hope that some day, after the acoustics have been improved, this organ will tell the listener what it really is."[14]

Recognizing the destructive results of undue compromise requires a fine balance between humility and firmness, between becoming either an artistic doormat or being arrogantly didactic. "You have one of the worst organs I have ever seen," he told an unbelieving committee in an important church (where, incidentally, he was not invited to build a new organ). With the same directness, he persuaded the authorities at Duke University that it would be hopeless to make a new organ in the chapel, unless the dead acoustics could be improved in advance (as was indeed done).

Into the American ferment

When Flentrop was introduced to the American organbuilding world in the 1950's, it was characterized by both restlessness and excitement. The forward-looking work of Donald Harrison at the Aeolian-Skinner Company in Boston and Walter Holtkamp in Cleveland was at its height. The post-war influx of recordings of European organs, as well as exposure of students to heretofore unavailable editions, the American recordings of such performers as E. Power Biggs, Carl Weinrich, Robert Noehren and others, plus the numbers of students journeying to Europe (especially Fulbright grantees, including Fenner Douglass and the writer), made for an exhilarating atmosphere. There was widespread interest in music of the seventeenth and eighteenth centuries, heightened by *collegia* established in the universities (including that led by Paul Hindemith at Yale and later, at the University of Illinois, under George Hunter), and this led to the instruments associated with the repertoire.

Walter Holtkamp's instruments for the Cleveland Museum (1946); Syracuse University (1950), where Arthur Poister was teaching; Donald Harrison's organs at the Germanic Museum at Harvard and at the Organ Institute in Methuen, Massachusetts (flourishing from 1947 for a number of years), with the rebuilt Walcker organ as its centerpiece: all epitomize the forces which combined to make musicians look with intense curiosity and excitement to Europe. This was also the period immediately preceding the rise of American builders interested in mechanical-action organs. Charles Fisk's first major instrument was to be completed in 1961, with Flentrop's blessings, as will be described later in this text.

It was into this ferment of ideas and energy that Flentrop came in 1956 with his address to the American Guild of Organists meetings. During the same decade, both his own organs and those of other European makers were to become widely known and respected in this country. Especially because of his missionary-like ability to teach others, it was to Flentrop that the majority of teachers and students began to look for guidance, encouragement, and, especially after the completion of the Busch-Reisinger organ at Harvard in 1958, for instruments. The early appearance of one of his organs in the most prestigious university in the country gave Flentrop an added notoriety and attraction. More important, his own temperament, combining conviction with an irrepressible bent to teaching, as well as the quality of workmanship in his instruments, made him into a veritable oracle in the eyes of those who would learn what the "classic" organ really was.

The concluding part of Flentrop's 1956 New York address summarizes his attitude of firmness tempered with humility: "I believe that we are now standing only at the beginning. We have learned only very recently how to recognize the fundamental principles . . . .But, just as the seven notes of the musical scale are subject to thousands of variations, so also the classical principles of organ-building have a very varied potential. I feel that we must always be alert for new applications of these principles and also, that we must remember that these principles are valid only when all are employed together, and not just when one is seized as a 'short cut.' Perhaps for each one of the valid possibilities that we try out, many others will be concealed from us. A good exchange between thoughtful American and European builders can be a good stimulus and it should help us to discover still-hidden potentialities . . . I would like to try to end this lecture by saying that I hope these nearer acquaintances will have the most happy effect both on our work and yours."

That latter hope, it may now be observed, was generously fulfilled in the succeeding two decades.

II. BEGINNINGS IN THE UNITED STATES: 1939—1959

In 1940 Dirk Andries Flentrop became director of the H. W. Flentrop Orgelbouw, which had been founded in Zaandam by his father Hendrik Wichert Flentrop in 1903. While the firm had built electric-action organs in the earlier years, there was also a strong interest in earlier instruments. This began when Hendrik Flentrop had observed the unfortunate results of the rebuilding (c. 1899) of an early-eighteenth-century organ by Duyschot in the Westzijderkerk in Zaandam, where he was organist. Just previous to World War II father and son had restored the Edam instrument (1934) and the beautiful Müller organ in the church at Beverwijk (1936). This was to become a hallmark for the future, when restorations became a major part of D. A. Flentrop's work. The first new slider chest made (1933) was for the existing organ in the Old Catholic Church, Krommenie. The war and the occupation of the Netherlands by the Germans drastically curtailed all activities, including organbuilding, with its requirements for metal and other supplies, to say nothing of shortages of food and fuel.

New York World's Fair, 1939

In 1939 Dirk Flentrop managed to bring an organ to the New York World's Fair (see Plate 7), just before the war closed all lines of transportation between the United States and north Europe. This first visit by the young Dutchman to the United States was filled with uncertainties about the friendliness of Americans. The erection of the instrument in the Netherlands Pavilion by Dutch organbuilders was questioned by the labor unions. In the ensuing confusion, work with "pipes" was labeled Plumber's Work, with commensurate standby wages to be paid. Workers were pressed upon him according to the materials of which the organ was made: not only plumbers, but electricians, carpenters and metalworkers as well. He was not allowed to do any work on the instrument, but only to supervise these helpers, who probably had never seen an organ before.

Their wages, including overtime, amounted to far more than the amount authorized by the Dutch government for transport, installation and the demonstration of the organ by a Dutch organist. Fortunately, the government, not Flentrop, paid the bill. Since the plumbers might have been involved with the final voicing and tuning, the builder was understandably in anguish. When their services were unexpectedly and urgently needed next door, his relief must have been immense: The Italian pavilion, which had a complicated waterfall on its roof, began to spring leaks. Fortunately for Flentrop, the plumbers were thus no longer available to help him, and he was allowed to proceed with tuning and regulation himself. But the discomfort generated by this reception into the

United States made it seem unlikely that the future held much for Flentrop in this apparently hostile country.

The New York World's Fair organ was among Flentrop's first mechanical-action slider-chest organs. Yet, it caused very little interest at the time among the Americans who saw and heard it; the time was obviously not yet ripe. Of this instrument Flentrop writes: ". . . New York was the beginning of our tracker slider chest organs. At that time, I didn't realize clear enough that for the pedal division, the same rules were as true as for the manuals. So, the New York pedal has electric action with a stopped 16 and 8, and an open 8 and 4 in the front. After the World's Fair, the organ came back to Holland, just a few days before the German occupation. It is now in a small church of a Rotterdam suburb."[15]

Shortly after his return from his first American trip, Flentrop wrote an article, giving his impressions of American organ building, as he then viewed it: "It is not to be expected in a country like the U. S. A., where it seems to have been forgotten that the organ, in the first place, must be capable of playing polyphonic music, that a radical change will come soon." ("Enige Amerikaanse Indrukken," *Organist en Eredienst,* 8e Jaargang, July/August, 1939.)

"How could I have dreamt at that time, that within less than twenty years, I would have built the Busch Reisinger organ?" he wrote to the author in March, 1981.

American visitors after the War

In any case, due to the war which was then beginning in Europe, there was a hiatus in communication with Americans until after the "Liberation" of May 5, 1945. The trickle of American students and teachers, which had begun in the late 1940's, became a torrent by the mid-1950's. Flentrop, along with other European makers, was being "discovered" by one after another of the eager young visitors. These musical pilgrims came not only to see new organs, but also to investigate old ones about which they had heard so much, and which were suited to the early music, editions of which were now pouring out of European publishing houses. The Fulbright exchange program was a significant catalyst in bringing together the Americans and Europeans, since it underwrote the substantial cost of living and travelling abroad. The large number of undamaged early organs in the Netherlands, and the presence of such teachers as Gustav Leonhardt (then at the Amsterdamsche Conservatorium) made Holland a mecca for organists and harpsichordists.

More often than not, these American zealots beat a steady path to the Flentrop workshops in Zaandam, where they were cordially received and provided with instructions, addresses and telephone numbers leading them to both old and new instruments throughout the country.

Often, when there was time and the visitors exhibited more than a tourist's interest in organbuilding, they were invited to the Flentrop house, nearby in Zaandam. There they were received by a gracious Marian Flentrop, who may well have offered more cups of coffee, *koekjes,* meals, and frequently lodgings as well, to tired Americans in those years than did the Nederland-Amerika Instituut!

Among the early visitors was Fenner Douglass, studying in Europe with the aid of a Fulbright award. Beginning his teaching at the Oberlin Conservatory about that time, Douglass spent much time in Zaandam with Flentrop, whom he had met in 1950. He had heard the Schnitger organ in the Laurenskerk in Alkmaar, restored by Flentrop in 1949. Speaking of the occasion Douglass recalls, "I knew the instrument would be fine, but was not at all prepared for the unearthly experience of hearing Bach's *Fantasia and Fugue in C Minor* played on the 1645 *Prestants.* It was probably a few weeks later, when [Simon C.] Jansen did a recital there that I met Dick. I so well remember *Christ unser Herr zum Jordan kam* on that program, played with the *Fiool di gamba* [reed stop] of the Hoofdwerk used as a cantus firmus in the Pedal. THAT was beautiful!"[16]

It was through Douglass's influence that the first Flentrop positief came in 1956 to Oberlin, after having been used for demonstration by Flentrop at the American Guild of Organists convention in New York. Other American university and conservatory teachers who visited the Flentrop workshops included Donald Willing (Trinity University), Melville Smith (Director of the Longy School in Cambridge), Hugh Porter (Union Seminary School of Sacred Music) and Frank Bozyan (Yale School of Music), among many others. In 1956 Margaret S. Mueller, in Europe thanks to the Fulbright program, visited the Flentrops, staying for a time at their house in Zaandam. Of this now legendary hospitality to American music students, Flentrop wrote to E. Power Biggs (August 17, 1956): "A few days ago we got a visit from Margaret Snodgrass, a student of Walcha. . . . we found it too bad that this girl had to stay all the time in cheap hotels or youth hostels . . . and we were thinking about our own daughter, travelling around abroad for a long time. So we asked her to stay in our home during the time she would see organs in the western part of Holland . . .." In 1957, through the influence of Margaret and her husband John Mueller, the first of three Flentrop organs arrived at Salem College.

First "classical organ"

These travels by American musicians, most of whom were also teachers, were to have a far-ranging effect. The beginning influx of Flentrop organs in the educational institutions mentioned above was a portent of what was to come in other schools during the next decade. Although no Flentrop instruments reached the United States until 1954, American visitors were impressed with the new work, as well as with the old. Flentrop's first full-blown effort in the "old style" was in the Hervormde Kerk in Loenen aan de Vecht, completed in 1950. The writer recalls, as do other visitors, being taken there by Flentrop himself in 1951. The ultimate influence of this lovely instrument alone on American organ-building could then hardly be imagined. The original organ by Bätz in 1787, housed in a single case, had been destroyed by fire. The new organ, with the main case based on the old single manual organ, and a Positief added by Flentrop, introduced the inquisitive foreigners to a fascinating tonal and tactile world.

Of the Loenen instrument Flentrop recalls:[17] "This Loenen organ I consider my first real classical organ. Not because it has trackers—I had made several organs with trackers and slider chests before the Loenen organ—but because it is an organ in which everything is present to make it into a fine musical instrument . . . to make it a pleasure for the eyes as well as for the ears."

And more recently he added, "This new Loenen organ case, based on the original design with only one manual, became possible thanks to the excellent collaboration with the architect in charge of the church restoration, the gifted Ferdinand B. Jantzen. . . . Without him and without his excellent design drawing . . . this organ would never have been made in the way it stands now."[18]

Students were frequently allowed, through Flentrop's recommendations, to use the new organ (1951) in the Kruiskerk in Amstelveen, a few kilometers from Amsterdam, for daily practice. They were also introduced to the restored Schnitger organ in Alkmaar, the Müller organ in Beverwijk, and soon also to the Schnitger organ at Zwolle (restored 1953-55). Later, others, including the Moreau organ at Gouda (restored 1960), were added to the list. American organ-builders as well as musicians were also welcomed by Flentrop. Charles Fisk came in 1957, as did Walter Holtkamp a few years earlier.

(text continues on page 39)

Plate 7. Netherlands Pavilion, New York World's Fair (1939)

Plate 8. Hervormde Kerk, Loenen aan de Vecht, Netherlands

Plate 9. Kruiskerk, Amstelveen, Netherlands

Plate 10. University Presbyterian Church, San Antonio, Texas

Plate 11. Typical six-stop Positief

Holpijp	8
Prestant	4
Fluit	4
Octaaf	2
Quint	3
Terts	1⅗
Mixtuur	III

Keyboard compass C - g‴.
Pedal compass C - d″.
Pedals permanently coupled to keyboard.
Holpijp, Fluit, and Quint divided at middle c.

Plate 12. Salem College, originally in "Old Chapel,"
Winston-Salem, North Carolina
(This photograph shows present location in studio.)

First organs for America

The first Flentrop instrument to appear in the United States was a four-stop Positief, acquired in 1954 by the University Presbyterian Church, San Antonio, on the recommendation of Donald Willing, then a faculty member at Trinity University. The church had first approached Flentrop about a small organ, and he had offered them an antique chamber organ, which later turned out to be so valuable that it exceeded their budget; also, Flentrop was not really in favor of selling it abroad. As Willing recounts, Flentrop then offered to make a new instrument for the same price. Describing this little instrument, Willing writes:[21] "We had quite a splash when it arrived; Otto Hoffman and I assembled it and had it playing in three hours, much to everyone's delight! First it sat in the large Skyline Room at Trinity University . . ., then in about 1¼ years was moved across the street into the new building that the church had provided itself . . .." The organ has been moved within the building several times since, but is still in use by the church, along with an instrument by Walter Holtkamp.

In 1957 the School of Music at Salem College acquired an organ of sixteen stops. Probably the favorable exchange of dollars for guilders, roughly one to four in those days, made importation an attractive alternative, not only from the Netherlands, but also from other European builders, notably Rieger in Austria and von Beckerath in Germany. Favorable prices were ultimately incidental, however. It became clear that these instruments interested musicians for three basic reasons: they sounded more lively, their action made it easier to control articulation and, most important, the repertoire sounded more convincing when played on them.

Correspondence with Douglass and Biggs

It was during this early period, before any Flentrop instruments had been imported, that the long-standing correspondence between Flentrop and Fenner Douglass began. Shortly after Douglass's return to the United States in 1951, they were already corresponding frequently both about the design of organs then being planned in Flentrop's workshop and about the possibility of collaboration with American builders, including, especially at that time, Walter Holtkamp.

By 1955, Flentrop was preparing talks to give to Douglass's students at Oberlin, then postponing the trip until 1956. He continued to keep his American friends informed of work going on in his shop and of the progress of restorations, writing to Douglass in October, 1955, "Zwolle is nearly finished now; it sounds marvelous. Come and hear it!" From 1951 onward, this lively exchange continued, sometimes with several letters per week, including a touching mixture of humor, family and household news, together with the most technical discussions of organbuilding. Drawings of actions, sketches of cases, descriptions of regulating procedures are all mixed with talk of the price of cheese, Old Dutch cookie boards, silverware, or the amount of linen needed for the American family's stay in Paris.

Not only Douglass, but also other leaders in the American organ world were in touch with Flentrop during this period. Probably the most crucial event in American organ history during the 1950's was the visit to Holland in the summer of 1956 by Mr. and Mrs. E. Power Biggs. Biggs had brought along recording equipment loaded into a Volkswagen bus, in order to "bring back aloud", as he

Plate 13. Dirk Flentrop and E. Power Biggs

put it, the sounds of early organs in Europe. The great Schnitger instrument at Zwolle, just restored by Flentrop, was one of the instruments he used for preliminary recording, as well as the Schnitger in the A-Kerk in Groningen and the sixteenth-century instrument in the small church in Oosthuizen (pumped for the occasion by the writer, who had been sent along as a guide by the Nederland-Amerika Instituut). Later, Biggs returned to record "Bach at Zwolle" as part of his survey of European organ sounds for Columbia Records. During this first trip, Biggs promptly introduced himself to Flentrop, who assisted him with introductions to various churches where there were interesting old organs that might be candidates for the forthcoming records.

The Busch-Reisinger Museum Organ

In 1957, an organ was ordered by Biggs from Flentrop for the Busch-Reisinger Museum at Harvard, to be used for both recordings and broadcasts. Despite the fact that the Columbia Broadcasting System discontinued the weekly Sunday morning programs (broadcast "coast to coast" since 1942) the following year, this instrument had enormous influence through recordings and recitals, as it continues to do.

The design of the Busch-Reisinger organ generated a detailed and excited correspondence between the organbuilder and Biggs. Its completion in 1958 was clearly a pivotal event both in Flentrop's American career and in American organbuilding history. Its importance is aptly summarized in the recently published history of the Flentrop Orgelbouw:[20] "It was an event of outstanding importance that Edward Power-Biggs [sic] took the initiative to have an organ based on classic principles built for the Busch-Reisinger Museum at Harvard University. This organ, . . . thereafter publicized extensively by Power-Biggs through concerts and recordings, introduced Flentrop's abilities to the United States, and especially since located in such an important place, it had a significant influence on the slowly changing attitudes regarding organ building and organ playing." A lecture, even when delivered before hundreds of the country's most distinguished organists, could be received and forgotten. The sound of an organ, both live and recorded, widely available to students and players, had a much more immediate effect. The generosity of Biggs, and the support of Charles Kuhn, Curator of the Museum, made the organ as accessible as possible. It was soon put into use for degree recitals by the New England Conservatory, with Biggs's blessings, and outside players were welcomed for frequent recitals.

The negotiations for the design of the organ may be followed in the letters rapidly flying back and forth between Zaandam and Cambridge. Growing excitement, generated by the prospect of introducing such an instrument to a wide audience for the first time in the United States, is evident on the part of both Biggs and Flentrop. On 22 September 1956, Biggs had written to Holland, asking about the possible design of an organ for the Busch-Reisinger Museum. Flentrop, on October 5, replied, ". . . It seems a wonderful idea to me!! I hope to find time next week to work on the design; the week after next week I am in

Plate 14. Busch-Reisinger Museum, Harvard University

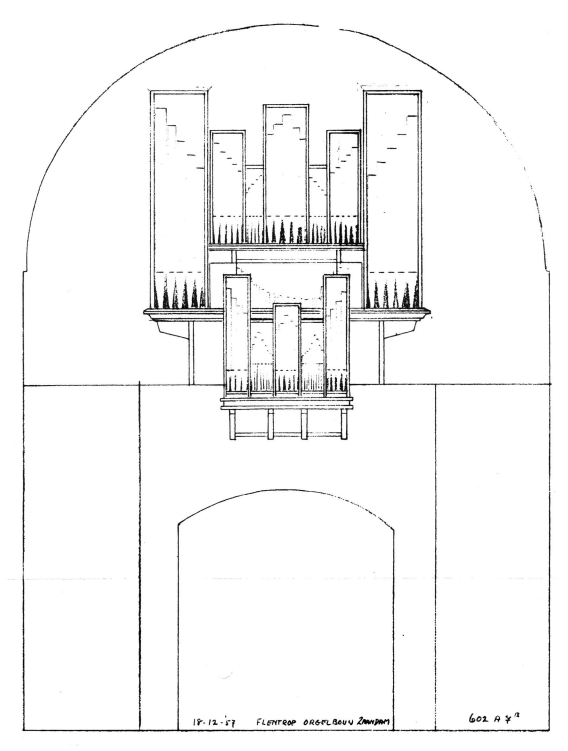

18-12-'57   FLENTROP ORGELBOUW Zaandam   602 A $\frac{2}{12}$

Plate 15. Busch-Reisinger Museum, Harvard University, Drawing

Sweden. If I don't find time next week, you have to wait another two weeks. Sorry. But I like it so much, that I think there will be time for it next week. For things you really like, you mostly find the time."[21] By October 9, Flentrop had "found time", sending Biggs a "design for an organ in the center of the gallery, which will be more satisfactory from an architectural point of view." The first proposal was for an organ of two keyboards, noting that "A third manual would only be possible when we make a Ruckpositiv" and that "The only right way is to place it on the floor of the gallery and that means we have to make rather important changes in the front wall of the gallery." The design quickly escalated to a three-manual scheme. Because no changes were permitted in the gallery itself, the Rugwerk was designed so that it rests atop the gallery front, held in place by its own weight, without being attached to the structure of the gallery. The main case also has no attachment to the floor or wall, being totally free-standing.

The most pressing initial problem was thought to be leaving floor space for instrumentalists in the gallery: ". . . if possible, up to eighteen players," wrote Biggs. The possibilities of locating the Pedaal on one side, away from the main case, as well as providing direct vision through the trackers (". . . and thus be able to have orchestra players all round!" Biggs suggested) were all discussed and rejected. Early on, Biggs assured Flentrop that "We want to be quite sure that the specification . . . as we finally settle it, is exactly as you want to build it! This is very important, so please say exactly what you prefer." Another result of these discussions was the dropping of an electric stop and combination action, initially proposed by Biggs. In December of 1956, Biggs wrote to Flentrop, "As you know, our great fault here has been to do things the wrong way, so that sounds are overloud and very strident on top. If your organ can have a persuasive, outgiving mellow quality, and a rich but never 'hard' ensemble, (yet very articulate in speech beginnings) I think it will just bowl people over! They will say THIS IS IT! It will be nothing less than an earthquake, for which America is ready *right now!*" [italics original]

Detailed conversations ensued about delivery time, the disposition of the organ, case design, the acoustics at the Museum, even the proper voltage for the blower. Interspersed were occasional humorous and domestic anecdotes. "Excuse me please, for the short letter, I am too busy having from Marian a special training in washing dishes, to show you how to do that very nice job!!!" wrote Flentrop in October 1957; and a letter from Mrs. Biggs in November of 1957 deals with lost suitcases, the power supply at the Museum and the price of Dutch cheeses.

The earlier Aeolian-Skinner organ at the Museum had been sold to Boston University and Flentrop supplied a six-stop Positief to test the acoustics and to give a better basis for making scales for the large organ. This Positief was also used in the interim before the arrival of *the organ,* as Biggs had begun to refer to the large instrument in their correspondence. This little instrument served, along with others, in a recording for Columbia Records, comparing the sounds of classic encased mechanical-action organs with American electric-action instruments. It was initially issued by Columbia as *The Organ* in 1958 and later reworked and issued (1969) in stereo as *The Organ in Sight and Sound.*[22]

Later the large organ was used in a recording of sonatas for two keyboard instruments by Antonio Soler, which became so popular that it was reissued by Columbia Records in several editions.[23] Biggs played the Flentrop instrument, while Daniel Pinkham played an eighteenth-century Dutch chamber organ made by Joachim Hess. This instrument, lent for the purpose by Charles Fisher, had come to the United States by way of Flentrop, who also provided advice for its restoration.

The Organ [in Sight and Sound] was a project of great importance for Biggs. He wrote humorously to Flentrop on May 23, 1958: "Civil war will probably break out here as soon as the record appears in August! I can hardly wait! Do you think I can get a job in Holland?

"Seriously, however, it will be wonderful to have this album 'published' at last. In giving it the de-luxe treatment Columbia are giving their vote-of-confidence in all the ideas and sounds it contains. They feel it may be one of their most important recording ventures. A real 'documentary' using the gramophone record in a truly educational way."

And further, speaking of Flentrop's forthcoming trip to the United States, "We look forward so much to your visit. Of course, if 'The Organ' record is out by then they may not let you in the country!"

Biggs, who referred to this as the "talking dog record," asked Flentrop to write a section of the accompanying booklet, which he agreed to do under the title "Designing and building the modern organ."

The final design (see Plate 15) for the Busch-Reisinger Museum organ arrived with a letter from Flentrop dated December 18, 1957, including his drawing numbered 602 A 7. Biggs replied on January 1, 1958: "The design is wonderful. As classic and balanced as Lübeck!" On July 21, 1958, Flentrop wrote that the organ would leave Rotterdam July 25, aboard the *Black Falcon*. Installation at the Museum began August 25.

Plate 16. E. Power Biggs, D. A. Flentrop, Charles Kuhn, Mrs. Biggs

Collaborations with American builders

During the mid-1950's, Flentrop was exploring the possibility of collaborating with American builders. On August 17, 1956, he wrote to Biggs that the firm of M. P. Möller had purchased several ranks of pipes from him, with the idea of voicing "un-nicked or nearly un-nicked pipes . . . He [Daniels] hopes that you will be able to play the organ and tell him what you are thinking about it . . .."

At this time, there was discussion about possible collaboration between Flentrop and various American builders, including Schlicker and Möller. In the same letter Flentrop observed, referring to Walter Holtkamp, "Today I got a very nice letter of Holtkamp, in which he said he was sorry I did not see more of his work . . .. And what you write, that Walter and I would complement each other is very true. . . . Walter would be the first man, because I know him already a long time and because, though he is sometimes a little bit difficult, I know he is very nice and he is absolutely an artist."

Much later, Flentrop recalled his experience with Holtkamp over several

Plate 17. Flentrop, Fenner Douglass, and Walter Holtkamp

decades: "I do not have the feeling that I have influenced Walter in any way. He had made himself before I learned to know him. He didn't like to be influenced at all; this may be the main reason he didn't change much and didn't want to make encased organs. Why should he? He made excellent instruments in his way and he didn't want to experiment in other ways with the risk of losing part of the excellence he had gained in his own specific way."[24]

About the initial Möller experiment, Biggs wrote on December 14, 1956, "And, by the way, in Hagerstown recently I tried the instrument made by Möller with your pipes. They are beautiful pipes, but I do feel that the results prove once again that it's impossible to obtain authentic tonal results on our conventional Pitman chests!"

During late 1958, Flentrop sought the advice of Charles Fisk about possible collaboration with the firm of M. P. Möller. Despite Flentrop's optimistic pursuit of several projects with that firm, no enduring relationship ensued. On November 5, 1958, Flentrop wrote to Mrs. Biggs, regarding overtures from Möller, "In a certain way, I think this will be possible, as long as they give me the freedom I need." And on November 10, 1958, he wrote to Fisk, "About Möller, I hope to do something to improve organbuilding in the USA . . . ." Later, July 25, 1959, Flentrop wrote to Fenner Douglass that he was making an organ for Möller to use as a demonstration instrument; "Moeller will make the pipes, according to my scales, and will voice and finish the organ . . . .. My hope is that working together with Moeller will have a stronger influence on the improvement of American organbuilding as the import of some European organs can have . . . .." The instrument in question eventually went to the University of Georgia at Athens.

Although these collaborations ceased almost before they had been tried, they constitute a typical example of Flentrop the evangelist. This was not a search for more business, since Flentrop was already exceedingly busy with his own organs and quoting long delivery times for new instruments. It was, quite simply, a "hope to do something to improve organbuilding in the USA."

It is fortuitous as well as typical that Flentrop's American work did soon proceed to collaboration with an American builder. After various discussions with Holtkamp and others, it was Charles Fisk who for a time was closely associated with Flentrop's first work for the United States, including maintenance of the Busch-Reisinger organ, located in Cambridge, not far from Fisk's shop. Fisk's predecessor at the then-named Andover Organ Company, Thomas Byers, had written to Flentrop in mid-1955, asking about a possible collaboration. Somewhat later, Fisk and Flentrop began to seek an arrangement to work with each other, with Fisk for a time representing Flentrop in the United States. This informal agreement was made in late 1958, with the clear understanding that Fisk would proceed with his own work at the same time.

The spirit of the collaboration was clear from the start. On November 10, 1958, Flentrop wrote to Fisk, "You don't represent AOC [Andover] or me; you advise them what is best for them. That might be me, might be AOC . . . .."

Throughout their lengthy correspondence, the mutual respect of the two builders is everywhere evident.

Among other projects, Fisk made alterations and adjustments to the wind supply of the organ in the Busch-Reisinger Museum. When Flentrop was approached in December of 1958 by Arthur Howes, organist of Mount Calvary Church in Baltimore, to build an instrument, his delivery time was longer than the church could abide. He agreed to act as a "consultant" and he recommended that Fisk be offered the job.

Flentrop recalls that the two builders met through the good offices of E. Power Biggs: ". . . he was the one who made me acquainted with Charles Fisk, just as he did with Hubbard and Dowd. Thanks to his acquaintance with Fisk, I told Arthur Howes that instead of me, because of our extremely long delivery time, he should ask Charles Fisk for the Baltimore organ. He would only do it if I took a certain responsibility; therefore, he wanted my name on the organ too."[25] Although the organ was designed and built under Fisk's supervision, the nameboard carries the inscription "Andover-Flentrop" in deference to Howes's request.

In the letters concerning the Baltimore organ, Flentrop wrote on April 11, 1959, "Indeed I would like very much to make this organ, but if this is impossible by the limits in time of delivery, please go ahead Charles, and make it. In that case I will give you all the help I can give." Fisk replied on April 27, ". . . I pray we may do it justice. For us, it will be our most important work to date and it will consume all our energies." In the same letter, he reported negotiations on Flentrop's behalf with Reynolda Presbyterian Church in Winston-Salem, North Carolina: "I think this is a very good situation, Dick. The truth is, I would rather build an organ here than in Baltimore."

Meanwhile, the correspondence between Fisk and Flentrop approached the prodigious. Fisk was careful to retain his own ideas, but equally careful not to offend his more experienced Dutch colleague. On December 21, 1959, when the scales for the Mount Calvary organ were sent to Flentrop for his suggestions and advice, Fisk wrote: "This whole pipe scale project has caused me to review thoroughly all the information on scales which I have . . .. The result of this is that I have used mainly my own judgement in trying to lay out an organ which is *consistent within itself.* This means that I have disregarded some of the advice given me by you and by others . . . and it worries me that you will think me disrespectful. . . . I would particularly like to know if there are points at which you think I am *really* wrong. Also, I would like to know which ideas you think are good, even though they vary from your standard practice . . .."

Although Fisk ceased to operate as a representative for Flentrop by the mid-1960's, their friendship and professional collaboration continued. In 1966, Flentrop asked for and received from Fisk the drawings for the mechanical combination action of the Baltimore organ. And in 1969, Fisk writes Flentrop a concerned letter about the fate of the organ designed for Carnegie Hall (but finally installed at the State University of New York at Purchase).

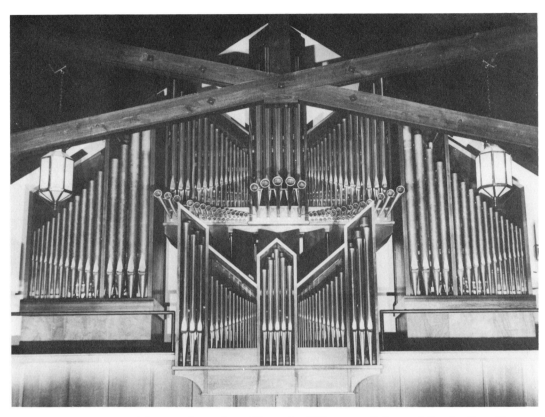

Plate 18. Reynolda Presbyterian Church, Winston-Salem, North Carolina

Plate 19. St. Mark's Cathedral, Seattle, Washington

Plate 20. St. Mark's Cathedral, Seattle, detail of keydesk

III. CONSOLIDATIONS: 1960—1969

St. Mark's Cathedral, Seattle, 1965

The organ in St. Mark's Cathedral, Seattle, dedicated September 19, 1965, was at that time the largest instrument Flentrop had built for America and marks a mid-point in Flentrop's American career. As is usual in such projects, negotiations went on for some time before and after the signing of a contract in January of 1962. Flentrop had provided two basic proposals: one was an instrument of modest proportions and the other, that ultimately adopted, was a complete scheme for the monumental cathedral building and its favorably reverberant acoustics. This, in Flentrop's opinion, required a 32' Pedaal and a Hoofdwerk with a 16' *Prestant* in the façade, as well as a full-length 16' *Trompet* (in this instance mounted horizontally in the façade).

Peter Hallock, organist and choirmaster of the Cathedral, had met Flentrop in 1961 while on a trip to inspect the organ in the Busch-Reisinger Museum. As happened later at Duke University, an electric action organ in need of expensive repair was a large part of the reason for seeking a new instrument. Because an organ was part of the completion plan for the Cathedral, and because of the influence it would have throughout the west, it was decided to build the larger of the two instruments. When the advice of E. Power Biggs was solicited, he wrote "Nothing in the world could be more wonderful . . . these rather elegant, articulate, and even slightly aloof sounds are perfect for church use, and have been so for hundreds of years." Biggs added, "Handel, Mendelssohn and others who played many times in St. Paul's Cathedral found nothing amiss!" But when the remarks were edited for publication, Biggs wrote back, ". . . I think the paragraph about Handel and Mendelssohn is better left out. . . . Someone may say that neither Handel nor Mendelssohn played the Episcopal service, which is of course true."[26]

It was at this time that the new organ for Carnegie Hall in New York was completed. It sat in storage for some time in Holland, awaiting delivery to New York. That this instrument was never installed there was a source of frustration and dismay to Flentrop, who worried that there might be some question about the quality of the instrument. Briefly the possibility arose that Oberlin College might arrange to purchase the organ; this came to naught, when the donor intended that it go to the State University of New York at Purchase, where it was ultimately installed (in 1977).

The forces which combined to cause Carnegie Hall to purchase a large instrument and then decide against its installation after it was constructed, still remain in the realm of mystery. There is no doubt, however, that musical opinions hostile to classic organ design were a factor. The manner in which an organ,

Plate 21. Warner Hall, Oberlin Conservatory, Oberlin, Ohio

Plate 22. Warner Hall, positief and keydesk

placed across the back of the stage used by orchestras, might affect the acoustics of the hall, also came up, although it seems hard to imagine that this was not considered before the decision was reached to have the organ built.

Of this instrument, Flentrop states:[27] "The original baroque case, designed according to Carnegie Hall's architecture, had to be changed when a modern stage decoration was advised for acoustical reasons. Again, in Purchase, changes were necessary, not all of them very favorable for the qualities of the original design."

Organs in Music Schools and Colleges

A growing list of centers for the training of organists now possess mechanical-action organs by both American and European makers for teaching and practice. A significant number of schools no longer employ electric-action organs at all for teaching. There is no question that the work of Flentrop was a major force in this direction, beginning with the first Positief at Oberlin, in 1956, and the first organ for Salem, in 1957. The list of organs built for the United States (See Appendix A) shows a total of 43 Flentrop instruments in educational institutions by 1977 among which the Oberlin Conservatory is surely the leader. A second six-stop Positief had arrived in 1959 (after temporary use in the Busch-Reisinger Museum). In 1962 Oberlin received five two-manual organs of eight stops; with two more, each of thirteen stops, coming in 1964; two more in 1969; and the Warner Hall instrument in 1974.

The breadth of this influence is striking; not only do Flentrop instruments appear in the older more famous institutions (the Juilliard School and the Eastman School each have an instrument, and the Yale School of Music has two), but in many small colleges widely scattered throughout the country. Flentrop also built two organs for Canada; for the Centre National des Arts, Ottawa, 1973: a Positief and a twenty-three stop instrument in the Concert Hall.

The influence of good instruments in smaller institutions is often all out of proportion to the size or notoriety of the college, especially when the refining of musical taste is viewed on a regional basis. Daily exposure to a responsive practice instrument may well do even more for the bright student than expert teaching. It is typical of this wide dispersion that one of the last instruments (1976) to come to a college during Flentrop's tenure was the nine-stop instrument for Warren Wilson College, a small and unusual school located at Swannanoa in the mountains of North Carolina.

The presence of Flentrop instruments has often been closely associated with a revival of intense organ study. A special example exists in the central South, where, beginning with the first Salem College organ in 1957 (through the influence of faculty members John and Margaret Mueller), there are now three Flentrop organs at the College, two Flentrop house organs in the town of Winston-Salem, and a three-manual Flentrop at Reynolda Presbyterian Church. By extension, at Duke University in Durham, there are two sizable Flentrop studio organs, a portable continuo organ (first used to test acoustics to provide scaling data for the Chapel organ), the monumental Chapel organ and two studio instruments by Charles Fisk.

More often than not, the presence of a successful instrument in a town has the ultimate effect of influencing others to follow suit, often with the work of an American builder. Thus, in Winston-Salem, at the North Carolina School of the Arts there is a three-manual instrument in the Recital Hall and several studio organs, all by Charles Fisk; at Ardmore Methodist Church, a handsome instrument by Fritz Noack; and a local builder in the Flentrop tradition, Norman Ryan, has produced a one-manual instrument for Nazareth Lutheran Church in the adjacent town of Rural Hall. Following the lead of Duke University there are also tracker instruments by Flentrop and by John Brombaugh in St. Stephen's Church and St. Paul's Lutheran Church, both in Durham. Over the long range, the influence of such a concentration of fine instruments, together with their intense use by students, can be expected to rival the larger and longer-established schools of music.

Spreading influences on musicians and builders

Slightly more than half of Flentrop's American instruments are in churches, where their influence on both musicians and the quality of church music continues to grow. It is more than speculation to hold that recent attempts to replace the organ with more "popular" instruments and repertoire have largely failed due to the emergence of a school of organ builders, typified by Flentrop, whose seriousness and integrity is unquestioned. Nor are many of these churches either large or urban, suggesting that the faint-hearted accusation of "elitism," occasionally levelled at thriving liturgical music projects, is either spurious or wrongheaded.

Since musical influences on clergy training are of obvious importance, it is arresting to observe that Flentrop was never invited to build an instrument for an American seminary chapel. This matter of lagging behind among seminaries deserves comment, because of the eventual influence which clergy have on the acquisition of instruments in the parishes. Just previous to the acendancy of mechanical-action instruments, Walter Holtkamp pioneered with several forward-looking seminary instruments. Although he did not continue his early (1935-36) experimentation with mechanical-action organs, among his electric-action slider-chest organs for seminaries were the following daring and successful attempts in the 1950's: Concordia Seminary, St. Louis (1953); General Theological Seminary, New York (1958); and the Episcopal Theological School, Cambridge (1956). It can be hoped that these instruments, advanced in their day, point to a renewal of concern, only temporarily interrupted by an infatuation with superficially accessible and ultimately boring musical sentimentality. That seminaries, along with many parishes, have sometimes been urged into extended liturgical experimentation is not to their discredit. But the initial risks in the renewed interest in good organbuilding have been taken by imaginative university chapels and individual churches. Recently acquired mechanical-action

Plate 23. Alabama College (University of Montevallo)

Plate 24. Virginia Intermont College, Bristol, Virginia

Plate 25. Warren Wilson College, Swannanoa, North Carolina

organs at the Yale Divinity School (by Fritz Noack) and the Virginia Theological Seminary (where new and revoiced pipework was supplied by Charles Fisk for an organ by Adam Stein, 1900) are among the brighter signs of a revival of concern in seminaries for the musical exposure of students.

A telling force for good instruments, just now beginning to be felt, lies in the sharpened discriminations of recent music school graduates who have been exposed to better equipment than their predecessors. The result is that these musicians seek positions in places where good instruments exist and also lobby for such instruments, when a new organ is to be purchased.

Just as the public use of the Busch-Reisinger organ heightened the interest in the "classic" organ, so the presence of the work of Flentrop and other European builders in chuches and colleges stimulated interest in the work of American builders, who were in turn influenced by the European organs. When the first Flentrop instrument arrived in San Antonio in 1954, only a tiny proportion of American organbuilding energy was concentrated on anything other than electric-action organs. There were no substantial shops devoted exclusively or even primarily to mechanical-action building. Otto Hoffman in Texas was certainly interested, and in 1956 he built a nineteen-stop instrument in Albany, Texas, for which he obtained pipes from Flentrop and the case of which was patterned after Flentrop's instrument in Groenlo in the Netherlands. Charles Fisk was beginning his work, and as has been seen, was supported and encouraged by Flentrop. Otherwise, a few imported organs constituted the beginning of the new emphasis in organ design, and a large percentage of the organists, although anxious to learn, were still skeptical of the new type of instrument; their skepticism was focused mostly on the mechanical action and lack of "conveniences." Electric-action instruments, with all of their eclectic compromises, were thought by the majority to be the wisest choice, except for unusual circumstances. After all, Walter Holtkamp's brief excursion in the mid-1930's into mechanical action had been all but ignored by most musicians, and was not pursued by Holtkamp himself.[28] These few small instruments were indeed a portent of what was to come, but they were not well-enough received to encourage Holtkamp to develop further mechanical-action designs, although he insisted on slider chests (with electro-pneumatic action) beginning early in his career. Holtkamp had also been frequently in touch with Flentrop, who recognized the artistic qualities in his work.

A special example of the reciprocal influence between Europe and America is the association between Charles Fisk and Flentrop. Not only did Fisk assist Flentrop by looking after the normal maintenance of the Busch-Reisinger organ in 1959. As discussed earlier, he also represented him for a time in the United States and received Flentrop's encouragement in the design and construction of the organ for Mount Calvary Church, Baltimore, in 1961.

Although other European firms, including Beckerath and Rieger, have doubtless influenced the younger American and Canadian builders, the Flentrop presence has been by far the strongest. It is also notable, that among the newer builders, a surprising number worked in the Fisk shop: Fritz Noack

(Georgetown, Massachusetts), John Brombaugh (Eugene, Oregon), David Moore (North Pomfret, Vermont), and Helmuth Wolff (Montreal). An interesting reference to Noack, especially in view of the independence later developed by him and the other former Fisk colleagues, occurs in a letter about the Baltimore organ from Fisk to Flentrop, December 21, 1959: "We have a new man, a young German of 24 years named Fritz Noack. He apprenticed with Beckerath and has worked with Becker and Arend & Brun-Zema [sic]. He is very full of enthusiasm and has many ideas — in fact, he is very intelligent and useful. His experience with mechanical action will be very useful to us." All of these makers have long since arrived at their own distinctive styles, after assimilating various influences of which Flentrop was by no means the only one. (Both Noack and Wolff, for instance, arrived on this continent after substantial experience with organbuilding in Europe, Wolff having spent time with Metzler in Switzerland as Noack did with the builders mentioned in Fisk's letter.)

Perhaps one of Flentrop's greatest services to American organbuilding has been his rigorous follow-up of instruments in this country. European builders normally take care to see that any problems with their exported instruments are promptly solved. Flentrop's especially rigorous insistence on this service had a widespread influence on the credibility of mechanical-action organs in general. His instruments always *worked* well and were therefore sounding proof that the classic design was viable. This does not mean that there were no problems, but that any difficulty after installation was satisfactorily and quickly solved. This was of particular importance with the very first instruments, subjected to American central heating, drastic humidity changes, and other conditions then unknown in Europe. The writer recalls taking a visitor to see the first Salem College organ shortly after its delivery, only to find the instrument totally disassembled and spread on the floor by Flentrop's men in order to replace the sliders with a new design developed for the low humidity caused by central heating. The initially mysterious wind problems in the Busch-Reisinger organ were rectified at once — or after long diagram-laden correspondence with Flentrop — by Fisk, with Flentrop's advice.

Plate 26. St. Anne's Church, Atlanta, Georgia

Plate 27. Christ Church, Oberlin, Ohio

Plate 28. First Unitarian Church, New Bedford, Massachusetts

Plate 29. Center United Presbyterian Church, Slippery Rock, Pennsylvania

IV. ARCHETYPES IN THE CLASSIC STYLE: 1970—1976

Unity in Design

Throughout Flentrop's American work, there remains a consistency in basic principles of design, principles which were already established and clearly set forth well before his 1956 speech in New York. Nonetheless, he retained an open curiosity, particularly when something was to be learned from new information turned up by a restoration project or by the work of another builder. The consistency is summarized remarkably in the dedication booklet for the Duke Chapel organ. It even calls to mind the straightforward statements of 1956: "The Duke organ is not a copy of any baroque organ. The Duke organ is entirely and especially designed for Duke Chapel, and according to the specific requirements of the Chapel. Modern organ building has rediscovered and adopted the principles of eighteenth-century organ building. These principles require a definite unity in tonal, technical and visual design. This means that together with designing the tonal structure, an architectural layout must be made according to the size of the building. The result is an organ in which *every part is related to every other.*"[29] [emphasis added]

Frustration in Cleveland, 1974

A remarkable example of Flentrop's concern for the integrity of his designs has to do with the organ for Trinity Cathedral, Cleveland. The organ was completed under the direction of Hans Steketee (1977), but the initial plans and preliminary sketch (see Plate 30) were made by Flentrop, the sketch (made during his first visit to the Cathedral) being dated 1972. After drawings were made and the instrument was designed in detail, a contract was signed. After this, Flentrop was astonished ("I was furious!" he recalled), to receive a brochure about the proposed organ, containing an architectural reworking of the final design, done by the Cathedral's architect, who had never conferred with Flentrop. It amounted to a total simplification of the Flentrop drawing, with the same general contours.

Commenting later about his frustration, Flentrop speaks of ". . . Cleveland Cathedral, which I think was the most difficult problem about a design we ever had in the States. In Holland and Germany, we had several problems, sometimes resulting in giving back the contract, and asking them to have the organ made by another builder, who was willing to listen to architects, instead of following his own way as a musical instrument maker."[30]

Flentrop went to Cleveland with Hans Steketee on November 19, 1974, to defend his proposal. In his notes for the meeting, he made the following points,

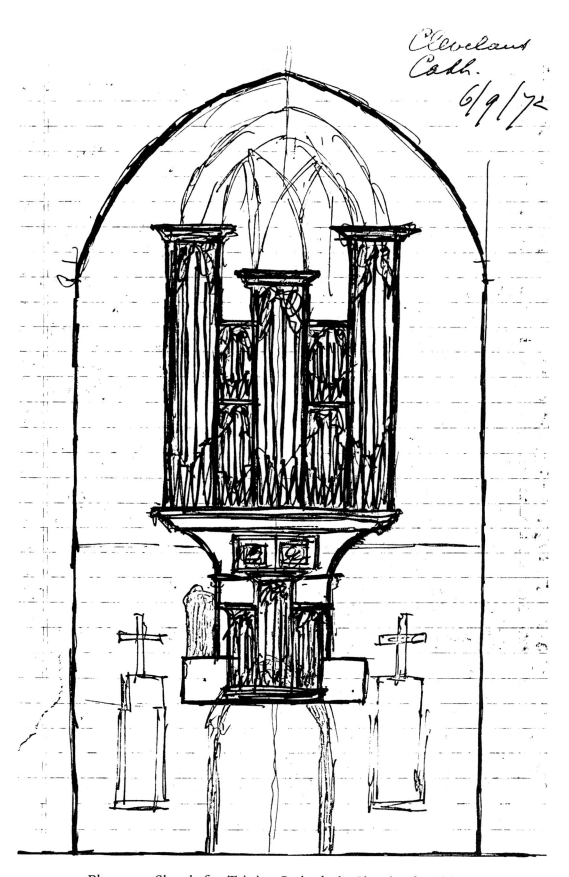

Plate 30. Sketch for Trinity Cathedral, Cleveland, Ohio

exemplifying the conviction required of the builder, if he is to retain artistic control: "From the day my father founded our firm in 1903, we tried (first my father, later together, since 1940 just myself, and in recent years together with Mr. Steketee), to make organs sound just as beautiful as they did in the past. During many years, being children of our time, we made the mistakes of the decadent period in organbuilding from the end of the 19th until the middle of the 20th century.

"It was not before 1950 that we made our first organ in which all necessary aspects of true organbuilding were represented. This happened to be the relatively small organ in the Protestant Church of Loenen, Holland, an organ not only with slider chests and tracker action, with well-made pipes in proper scaling and voicing, but also and most important with a true, a traditional organ case.

"After Loenen we made several organs according to the principles we had developed, but also many times we were influenced by architects to change our designs and to modernize our plans. Every time we did, we felt afterwards that the sound, and also things like action and wind supply would have been better, if we had strictly followed our principles. So, finally, we came to the point to have so much faith in our work that we decided to make only organs in the way we want to make them, the way we know best . . .."

He then referred to the contract for the organ, and continued, ". . . To my great surprise, in July 1974, I found in the mail two drawings with similar pipe arrangements as my design, and a third one somewhat later with a different pipe arrangement. All these new drawings, however, were based on plywood construction, regular pipes shades and no mouldings. I found, and still find these suggestions not acceptable.

"At first sight this may not seem important to you, but it will mean that an organ we would make according to the principles of your drawing will never, can never sound and play as well as an organ in which we are free to make it entirely to a design that we feel is the best . . .. Everything in an organ is closely related to sound and action. Every step neglecting these relations means that we lose in quality. I am sure you don't want that and I ask you as stringently as I can: 'Leave the design entirely to me and you will get the best I can make.' "

Wisely, the organ was finally built according to Flentrop's design.

Case, wind-supply, stop actions: advances

The beginning of the 1970's is a good point at which to assess what was learned from earlier instruments and restorations and how it was applied to the design of later organs in the United States. Flentrop's basic attitude to the importance of the organ case as a reflecting shell, as well as an architectural housing, remained constant. However, the decoration of his cases sustained interesting changes. The 1965 Seattle organ is elegantly designed in a frankly contemporary idiom (with drawings largely by Hans Steketee); the Salem College Recital Hall (1965) and the Busch-Reisinger (1959) instruments exhibit equally clean façades, without pipe shades or other decor, giving neither an antiquarian nor particularly adven-

Plate 31. Recital Hall, Salem College, Winston-Salem, North Carolina

Plate 32. Recital Hall, Salem College, detail of keydesk

Plate 33. Christian Science Church, Batesville, Arkansas

Plate 34. First Presbyterian Church, Concord, North Carolina

turous appearance. As early as 1960, in the organ for Batesville, Arkansas, Flentrop produced a case for an American church which was clearly decorated in the manner of the eighteenth century. Of this instrument, Flentrop wrote to Douglass from Batesville, September 8, 1960; "It is too bad that you can't come to Batesville. That organ with its 19 registers sounds especially beautiful!! And also, the case and the façade, in colonial Georgian style are very beautiful, although I prefer a 'contemporary' design." This earlier instrument suggests the shift in case ornament, which was to emerge fullblown in the later instruments, such as the Warner Hall organ at Oberlin (1974); the Presbyterian Church, Concord, North Carolina (1975), again in the Georgian manner; and Duke Chapel (1976), best described together with the Oberlin organ as classically Dutch. In fact, Douglass had written about the Duke design (not so much about the case as the disposition) on July 28, 1970, ". . . the whole thing looks now (1) much better balanced, and (2) really DUTCH!" It was also about this time that Flentrop became convinced that pipe shades were more than decoration and that they had a salutary effect on the diffusion of the sound of the organ, helping prevent concentration of higher frenquencies by distributing them more evenly.

About the importance of pipe shades, Flentrop wrote concerning the Duke Chapel organ, "Pipe shades cover the openings at the tops of the front pipes and help to blend the sounds of those pipes with those of the interior pipes. Like the placement of the front pipes, the pipe shades also follow an irregular mode—being of many different shapes. This, too, however, is functional rather than decorative, for the irregularity of the pipe shades prevents them from giving preference to certain overtones. Similarly, the intricate shapes of the mouldings help to diffuse the sounds into all parts of the Chapel."[31]

The matter of providing the best possible wind supply had long occupied Flentrop's attention, as mentioned earlier in discussion with Fisk. This concern was shared not only by Fisk, who gave it special prominence (insisting on a single large reservoir with no *schwimmers* in the 1961 Baltimore organ), but also by other builders in the United States and Canada, including Noack, Wolff and Brombaugh.

At least as early as 1957, Flentrop was using large bellows reservoirs, seeking a solution which combined steady wind with a freer, "floating" supply. This was applied to instruments for the United States as it was developed, the first example being an instrument for the Woestduin Kerk in Amsterdam and the first American one being Reynolda Presbyterian Church in Winston-Salem, North Carolina, 1961.

Fisk, having heard of the Amsterdam instrument, wrote Flentrop on September 28, 1959, ". . . I would certainly appreciate any opinions you have on this matter of the wind, any details or suspicions you may have. As you know, I am much concerned with it myself, and have been for a long time. If you can keep me informed in detail as to your current thoughts about the effect of conductor size and length, bellows size, pallet box size, etc. I will be everlastingly grateful, and I shall certainly be glad to give you the benefit of any paltry thoughts I may have on the subject." (Despite Fisk's modesty, he managed successful solutions providing freer wind, based on early practices, from 1961 onward.[32])

In his 1956 New York lecture, Flentrop had noted that wind supply was kept steady by regulators *(stabilisators)* "built into the bottom of the chest itself." In that time, Flentrop (and the other builders involved with the restoration of early organs) were urged by fearful advisors to ensure that wind was even *too* steady for the best musical results, as is noted in the seventy-fifth anniversary booklet of the Flentrop Orgelbouw: "The firm demand of the Organ Commission for attention to the pressure in the chest, with an eye to the altered climate conditions, was the cause for frequent use of this modern solution."[33] The return to larger, freer, reservoirs, with less concern for utterly "unshakeable" wind, was an advance in the direction of the early principles of winding, which have an integral relation to the sound of the pipes.

Regarding an improved wind supply, Flentrop wrote to Douglass on January 12, 1970, ". . . What about the blower giving a stream of turbulent air instead of a bellows activated by manpower. Isn't this kind of wind supply like a singer with a hole in his chest and a small blower giving air in his lungs? I discussed this at length with Charles Fisk . . .. I asked him to think of a kind of construction where the blower is disconnected after the bellows is full. I am working at it and we promised each other to let us know about possible results. Just today I sent a letter to Charles, though I didn't yet find the solution." And later, speaking to organbuilders:[34] ". . . We realized that the perfectly stable wind supply we had learned to make did not satisfy us anymore. We wanted to have more expressivity. We experimented in old and new organs and by doing this, we came to the conclusion that the large V-shaped bellows or feeders—not having reservoirs—together with rather narrow windtrunks gave better results . . .."

In addition to the case and its decor, as well as the wind supply and action, attention was also paid to the dispositions and scales of organs destined for differing acoustical environments and architectural spaces. The basic principle held firm: there must be an overall unity in the design and each division of the organ, insofar as its size permitted, must be an entity, with its own flue chorus and appropriate reeds, with pitches related to the total scheme.

Thus, the Seattle organ has a 32' *Prestant* in the Pedaal, with a 16' *Prestant* in the Hoofdwerk, with a Bovenwerk of 8', 8' Rugwerk and 4' Borstwerk. The Duke Chapel organ, larger in total number of registers, has a 16' Pedaal *Prestant*, with *Prestant, Bourdon,* and *Bombarde,* all of 16' pitch, in the Hoofdwerk. At Duke, there was special concern that scales be wide enough to produce a full sound in the building. There are also reeds of French construction—an important reminder that Flentrop's background includes not only north European ideas, but also experience with instruments in the French and other styles. He made special investigations in France and Spain, including a trip to France in connection with the design of the Duke organ. In Holland itself there exist early instruments by builders much influenced by French ideas, including the Séverin

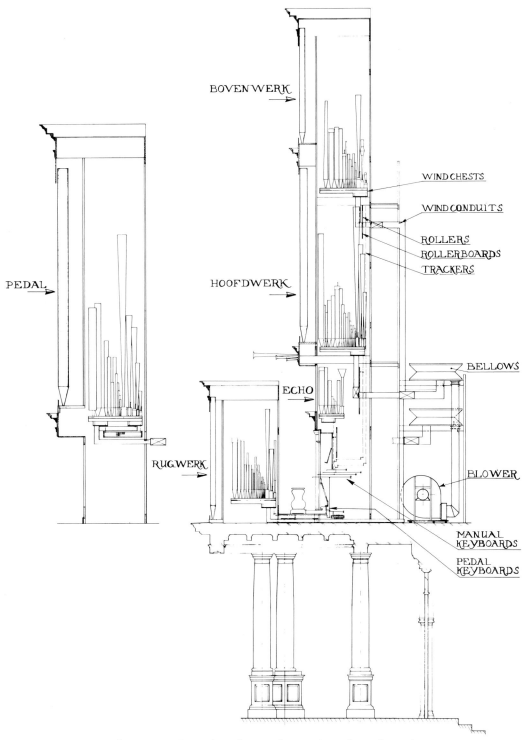

BOVENWERK →

WIND CHESTS

WIND CONDUITS

ROLLERS
ROLLERBOARDS
TRACKERS

PEDAL →

HOOFDWERK →

BELLOWS

ECHO

RUGWERK →

BLOWER

MANUAL
KEYBOARDS

PEDAL
KEYBOARDS

Plate 35. Drawing for Duke University Chapel

organ at Maastricht and the Moreau organ at Gouda, both of which have been restored by Flentrop.

The Seattle Cathedral organ of 1965 (four manuals, 55 registers) can be instructively compared with the two later instruments of similar proportions: those at Oberlin Conservatory (1974, three manuals, 44 registers) and Duke Chapel (1976, four manuals, 66 registers). The Seattle organ has wind regulators built into the chests, a practice more or less normal for Flentrop's earlier organs in the United States. It also has electric stop and combination action, unusual for Flentrop, but occasionally employed (with misgivings) in a few organs in the late 1960's. Seattle came only slightly earlier than the largest instrument ever made by Flentrop, that for the Rotterdam Concert Hall ("De Doelen"), made in 1968 with seventy registers. The Seattle instrument was the first large organ in which Hans Steketee, who joined the Flentrop firm in 1958, had an important voice.

The organ intended for Carnegie Hall, New York, and the Rotterdam Concert Hall organ employed electric stop action, partly due to pressures generated by their being "concert" organs, on which literally unpredictable demands might be made. It was not long after, however, that Flentrop firmly decided that electric stop actions were incompatible with good design, partly because they tempted the organist to use the instrument in an orchestral or some other unidiomatic way. In his own words, "A telephone exchange mechanism does not belong in a musical instrument."

Instruments for Oberlin (1974) and Duke (1976).

Coming near the end of Flentrop's tenure as *Directeur,* both the Oberlin Conservatory and Duke University Chapel organs are of special interest, especially since they are of sufficient size to enable the builder to carry out a large scheme completely. The aim was to design each of these instruments as faithfully as possible in the late-seventeenth-century style, as it was known in the Netherlands. This Netherlandish style, as reflected in the instruments, differs from both Germanic and French ideas of the same period, and is, in part, a merging of the two, along with features peculiar to the lowlands builders.

In both organs, Flentrop's interest in consulting with experienced musicians was a significant factor in the ultimate design. As with several other organs for America, the advice of Fenner Douglass was important in the planning and finishing of the instruments for Duke and Oberlin.

There was extended discussion concerning some of the reed stops for Duke Chapel. Flentrop describes it thus: "For a situation like the one at Duke, where the idea came up to include several French reeds, Fenner, Hans, Siem and I went to France, studied French organs and especially French reeds, and decided there what was best to do. The discussions we had were sometimes quite hectic but were finally leading to the best we could make, even if it is not as 'French' as wanted. I still doubt if more 'French' could be possible with anti- or un-French acoustics like Duke."[35]

Since the Duke organ enjoys an ideal location in the west gallery of a now-

reveberant church, it is an appropriate—even architypal—statement of what
Flentrop thought optimum for a large instrument in this style. His statement
about this organ, quoted earlier, confirms the regularly-stated principle that the
unity of the whole concept is paramount "in tonal, technical and visual design."
In the same publication Fenner Douglass writes, "The building was no artful
deceit. It was the real thing, right down to every handcarved detail of stone construction . . . How fitting and artistically consistent that Duke Chapel should
become the musical soundingboard for an organ rooted solidly in the great
liturgical traditions. The need for a seasoned artist-builder was met with the
choice of Dirk Flentrop, a native Lowlander, experienced in the restoration of ancient instruments and a man with a lifetime of exposure to the cross-currents between French and German national styles.

"There was no whimsical trait to the new Flentrop organ. Like the modern
harpsichord of surpassing quality, a violin, recorder, pianoforte, it owes its
physical outline, its interior layout, materials and techniques of construction,
even its decoration to an established historical prototype, for which a great
literature exists. The intention is to reproduce music of a particular period and
scope as faithfully as might be possible in the 1970's."[36]

Already, the continuation of the firm was kept in mind, and the younger Hans
Steketee, well past apprentice days, became more important in the solution of
design and other organbuilding problems. Of their work together over twenty
years, Flentrop observed, "I wanted to give him the freedom to develop into a
good organbuilder, rather than telling him how everything must be done."
Steketee has independently noted that he indeed felt free to find his own way,
"even when we did not agree."

When the Flentrop Orgelbouw celebrated its seventy-five year Jubilee in 1978,
Flentrop had already retired. He is cited frequently in the text of the booklet
Vijfenzeventig Jaar Flentrop Orgelbouw, as are his organs and restorations in the
United States and Europe. Careful reading of the text suggests that the attitudes
and thoughts of his succesor shape much of the philosophy set forth there, even
though the two builders share the same basic conviction.

The idea of "unity" as the essence of any good design in a given style
dominates Flentrop's thoughts on that subject in an almost religious fashion. It is
reiterated in his description of the re-construction (1976) of the Duyschot organ
of 1712 in Zaandam, located only a few hundred meters from his workshop. Since
this organ had been completely disfigured by unsympathetic work by another
firm (about the time his father became an organbuilder) the opportunity to
return it to its original splendor was a special one. He writes, "This work of
reconstruction was not done to have just the pleasure of copying an old historical
organ. No, it had to be done that way to make the still-existing front, together
with the new organ interior, into a unity. A unity, an entity, with the sole and
only purpose to serve the music, to make the organ a lively, exciting and
beautiful musical instrument."[37]

V. RESTORATIONS IN MEXICO

Not only because D. A. Flentrop was among the first and most resolute advocates of responsible restoration of early organs, but also because his largest single restoration project was done in North America, it is in order to include a brief description here. The work is the restoration of the two great organs in the Metropolitan Cathedral of Mexico.[38] As will be seen, this challenge was one of monumental proportions, for which his earlier restoration experience in North Europe as well as in Portugal served him well. This condensed account will also give the reader an indication of the care and frustration involved in any major restoration of an early organ, as well as a feeling for the enormity of this unique undertaking.

Despite Flentrop's experience with organs in a similar style in Evora Cathedral (1967), Oporto Cathedral (1970) and Coimbra University (1972) in Portugal, the Mexico project presented difficulties as unusual as they were frustrating.

First, the two organs in Mexico Cathedral rival in size anything to be found in Spain or Spanish America, making disassembly and shipment a special problem. Because the traditional organbuilding crafts do not at present exist in Mexico, it was necessary to ship both instruments (except for casework) to the workshops in Holland. They went by air — seventeen tons!

Second, a serious fire in the choir of the Cathedral in January of 1967 had damaged the carving of the façades and melted most of the pipes mounted in the case fronts, including many of the façade reed resonators. Worse, after the fire, unauthorized people had gained access to the interior of the organs, causing further damage by mishandling of the pipework and mechanism.

The third and most tantalizing difficulty was the ultimate pressure to complete the project in the shortest possible time, due to strictures imposed by Mexican government funding arrangements, which make it extremely risky to carry over such a project from one administration to another. Negotiations were begun with Flentrop in 1973, and he submitted a five-year plan for the work. The Mexican response to this did not come until September 1975, together with the urgent request that the work be completed by the end of the current presidential term in December 1976! This deadline was impossible to meet, and the completion in 1978 required diverting much of the Flentrop staff from other projects in order to finish the work in such a short time.

The historical and musical importance of the Mexico Cathedral instruments is extraordinary. They are the most imposing early organs still existing on the North American continent, and they had been out of effective use for decades. Although numerous smaller early instruments survive, albeit usually in unplayable condition, many other large eighteenth-century instruments in Mex-

Plate 36. Mexico Cathedral, nave façade of north organ

ico have either been totally lost, or as in the splendid cathedrals of Morelia and Puebla, drastically altered or replaced except for the façades. Mexico City alone now has, for the first time in modern times, appropriate vehicles for the performance of the great Spanish organ repertoire, which perhaps more than any other, demands the specific sonorities and effects which are peculiar to the Spanish organ.

For Flentrop, these restorations represent not only the most formidable ones of his career, but also as director of the Flentrop Orgelbouw, the last ones. Together with the Duke Chapel organ, which, not incidentally, contains Spanish-style trumpets mounted horizontally in its façade—these organs were completed just before his retirement, and finally inspected by him in October 1978.

To better understand the complexity of these restorations, it is helpful to mention the characteristics peculiar to organs in the high Spanish style of the late seventeenth and early eighteenth centuries. Instruments in Mexico are entirely in this genre—many constructed by Spaniards brought to Mexico for that purpose—and they differ from the more well-known Germanic, French and Dutch styles, especially in the following dramatic ways:

1) Spanish instruments, after the "invention" of horizontally-mounted façade reeds in 1677 by Hechevarría, are totally dominated by brilliant trumpet and other reed stops, mounted horizontally in the façade of the organ. Cathedral instruments normally have double-fronted cases, speaking into both the choir and an ambulatory. Hence, there are two sets of *clarines* registers, as in both organs in Mexico Cathedral.

2) All registers run through only half the keyboard compass, either from the bass to middle c or from middle c-sharp up in the treble.

3) There usually are no pedals. If pedals exist, they normally have a range of an octave or less, permanently coupled to the main keyboard. In very large organs, there may be independent pedal registers, in addition to the coupling. In the Mexico Cathedral organs, there are independent flue and reed stops (with 16, 8 and 4' pitches drawing together) plus an *added* bass octave from CC in the main keyboard, coupled to the pedals.

4) Special effects abound, including bells, bird sounds and imitations of drums and other percussions.

5) A *caja de ecos,* or simple swell box with a hinged lid rather than shutters, containing treble registers including a *corneta* of five ranks, is a regular component of the design.

6) Nearly all the bass pipes are located elsewhere than on the main chest, with wooden groove-boards and lead tubes conducting the wind from the chest.

7) The case serves primarily as a profusely ornamented façade, usually rather deep and open at the top.

8) In the Cathedral organs, located above the floor of the choir, the wind supply is on top of the organ, there being too little room below. This partly explains false front pipes on the top level, since they screen the wind supply from view.

9) Where there is a second or *Cadereta* division, higher pitched stops and a

single 8' register (and sometimes only the treble of an 8' register) are in the Cadereta case, with other 8' and 4' stops inside the main case on floor level, where chest and pallet box are also located.

To give an idea of the size of the organs, Flentrop repaired approximately 6400 pipes; 8200 square feet of sheep leather was required for repair inside the windchests and for releathering gigantic bellows. A ton and a half of metal from the ruined façade pipes was melted down for recasting, while samples were taken to reproduce metals for other missing pipes. The main cases of the organs (which also contain *caderetas,* located in *Rückpositiv* position) are approximately 56' high by 30' wide. The North organ has 90 registers, the South organ, 85. Each of the organs has fifteen reed stops mounted horizontally in the façades.

Among the factors common to organ restorations, the following presented special problems with the Mexico Cathedral work:[38] Much of the pipework was missing, due in small measure to fire damage and in large measure to vandalism after the fire. Of the pipework, 3861 pipes were in "good to rather good condition;" while 929 were damaged, but restorable; 1779 pipes had disappeared altogether. For repair and replacement, new pipes were made of metal containing the same amount of tin and lead (determined from laboratory samples) as were the originals. Scales for such missing pipes were determined by many considerations, including comparison to the remaining pipes of a register, available windchest space, measurements of pipe rack-boards. Such data produce appropriate measurements for diameter, mouth width and cut-up, toehole, languid and metal thickness. A diagram was then made from each rank, from which measurements for missing pipes could be determined.

Wooden pipes are less easily destroyed than metal ones, although most required re-gluing, repair of cracks and recovering with linen, since the original finish had deteriorated. Metal pipes were straightened with mandrels and soft hammering, mouths reshaped, and seams soldered.

Numerous cracks in the windchests were repaired with sheep leather and the bellows and other parts of the wind supply had to be totally re-leathered, as did all chest surfaces on either side of the sliders, and the pallets inside the chests. The existing key and stop action was restored and regulated and new parts were made to replace those missing. Except for restoration of case carvings, which was done in Mexico by staff of the *Instituto Nacional de Antropologia y Historia,* all the shop work took place in the Flentrop workshops in Holland. When the instruments were returned to Mexico, final voicing and regulating was done by the Flentrop men, after the instruments were reassembled in the Cathedral.

Flentrop notes one striking aspect of the windchest construction, which is the very ancient and unusual practice of making a chest from solid wood, with grooves actually cut into the wood itself, rather than the usual method of making the note channels of several separate pieces of wood. A similar construction exists in some early north European organs, in the "bamboo" organ in Manila, and doubtless in Spain.

During the process of disassembly and restoration (under the direction of Cees van Oostenbrugge of the Flentrop staff), considerable evidence appeared, strongly suggesting that both organs were the work of the same man, José Nassarre, in 1735, and that both organs were built in Mexico. Mexican historians are still seeking evidence which will clarify the relation between the present organs and whatever instruments preceded them in the Cathedral. There was a substantial earlier instrument, at least by 1696, in Mexico Cathedral, which instrument was probably absorbed into the present instruments by Nassarre. There is also a signature in the North organ originally thought to have been older that the South instrument, which reads: "Dn. Joseph Nassarre fecit ano 1735 . . .." together with a second signature recording repairs by José Perez de Lara in 1817. Further documentation for the earlier organ in the Cathedral consists of a letter to Spain from the *Cabildo,* dated 1688, requesting ". . . un organo grande con su cadereta . . .;" a request from Tiburcio Saenz, circa 1695, to be paid for work done in setting up the organ. The 1735 organs are reported in the *Gaceta de Mexico* for October 23, 1736.[39]

Plate 37. Flentrop Workshop, Zaandam, Holland

Plate 38. Flentrop Restoration Shop, Wapenveld, Holland

VI. EPILOGUE

Choosing a successor

In the best efficient Dutch manner, Flentrop arranged his retirement as *Directeur* of the Flentrop Orgelbouw, first by turning the direction over to an energetic and exerienced successor, Hans Steketee, and second, by insuring that the future of the firm would be determined by organbuilders rather than by stockholders. ". . . Since January 1st 1978 I am in every way out of the firm. *All* shares are now owned by employees of Flentrop Orgelbouw and by Hans. It is my hope that with this arrangement the continuity of the firm will be secured for a long period of time. Anyway, there is now a strong financial base and no risks that shareholders can do things against a good organbuilder's philosophy. This of course could happen in situations where shareholders have only a financial interest and no interest in organbuilding . . .."[40]

Honors at home and abroad

There is no doubt that Flentrop was accorded a healthy respect by his musical and organbuilding colleagues, as soon as his work became known in the United States. More formal accolades were somewhat later in coming, but they were appropriately formidable. In 1968, he was awarded an honorary doctorate by Oberlin College; in 1976, Queen Juliana conferred the title of Officer of the Order of *Oranje Nassau*. In the same year, Duke University awarded an honorary doctorate on the occasion of the dedication of the organ in the university chapel. In 1978, he was made an honorary member of the American Institute of Organbuilders. These honors are, however, worn by a modest gentleman, whose American friends occasionally playfully address him with formal Dutch titles (*Hoog Geleerde Weledelgeboren Heer,* doubtlessly as badly spelled as pronounced)—worn with predictable deference, dignity and, no doubt, with quiet humor as well.

Plate 39. Dirk and Marian Flentrop

Plate 40. Dirk Flentrop (Washington, D. C., 1980)

APPENDIX A: LIST OF ORGANS
IN THE UNITED STATES OF AMERICA BUILT
BY FLENTROP ORGELBOUW B. V., ZAANDAM
(to September, 1977)

1954

San Antonio, Texas	University Presbyterian Church	1m	5s	6r

1956

Oberlin, Ohio	Oberlin Conservatory Practice organ	1m	6s	7r

1957

St. Cloud, Minnesota	Holy Angels R. C. Cathedral (later moved to school)	1m	6s	7r
Winston-Salem, N. C.	Salem College "Old Chapel"	2m	16s	21r

1958

Montevallo, Alabama	St. Andrew's Church	1m	6s	7r
Cambridge, Mass.	Busch-Reisinger Museum	3m	27s	33r
Chicago, Illinois	House organ	1m	4s	4r

1959

Fayetteville, Arkansas	University of Arkansas	1m	6s	7r
Pittsburgh, Penn.	St. Mary's Church	1m	6s	7r
Oberlin, Ohio	Oberlin Conservatory Practice organ	1m	6s	7r

1960

Montevallo, Alabama	Alabama College (for teaching purposes)	2m	13s	17r
Batesville, Arkansas	First Church of Christ, Scientist	2m	19s	26r
Fort Smith, Arkansas	St. Scholastica's R. C. Academy	1m	6s	7r
Winston-Salem, N. C.	House organ	2m	7s	8r

1961

Winston-Salem, N. C.	Reynolda Presbyterian Church	3m	30s	39r
Oberlin, Ohio	House organ	2m	9s	10r

1962

New Haven, Conn.	Yale School of Music			
	Two practice organs	2m	6s	7r
Oberlin, Ohio	Oberlin Conservatory			
	Five practice organs	2m	8s	9r
Bluffton, Ohio	Bluffton College			
	Practice organ	2m	8s	9r
New York, New York	Noah Greenberg, Pro Musica			
	Antiqua, Two small Positiefs	1m	1s	1r
	Positief (Gedeckt 8, Koppelfluit			
	4, Principal 2, Mixtuur II,			
	Kromhoorn 8)	1m	5s	6r
Sudbury, Mass.	House organ	2m	9s	11r
New York, New York	House organ	2m	9s	10r

1964

Oberlin, Ohio	Oberlin Conservatory			
	Two practice organs	2m	13s	16r
Oberlin, Ohio	Christ Church	2m	11s	13r

1965

Seattle, Washington	St. Mark's Cathedral	4m	55s	76r
Winston-Salem, N. C.	Salem College, Recital Hall	3m	25s	34r
Collinsville, Conn.	First Congregational Church	2m	18s	28r

1966

Atlanta, Georgia	St. Anne's Church	2m	25s	33r
San Diego, California	Portatief	1m	1s	1r
New Bedford, Mass.	First Unitarian Church	2m	25s	31r

1967

New York, New York	Carnegie Hall (never installed)			
	see under 1977, State University			
	of New York, Purchase			
Palo Alto, California	All Saints Church	1m	7s	8r
Greenville, Pa.	Thiel College	1m	6s	7r

1968

Evanston, Illinois	Northwestern University	2m	9s	10r
Charlotte, N. C.	House organ	2m	9s	10r
Eugene, Oregon	University of Oregon	2m	8s	9r
Rochester, New York	University of Rochester			
	Eastman School of Music	2m	8s	9r

1969

Stillwater, Oklahoma	House organ	2m	11s	12r
New York, New York	Juilliard School	2m	14s	17r
Slippery Rock, Pa.	United Presbyterian Church	2m	18s	22r
Branford, Connecticut	First Congregational Church	2m	33s	47r
St. Petersburg, Fla.	Florida Presbyterian College	2m	15s	18r
Palo Alto, California	All Saints' Church	2m	18s	24r
Denton, Texas	North Texas State University	2m	3s	3r
Oberlin College	Oberlin Conservatory			
	Two practice organs	2m	3s	3r
Knoxville, Tennessee	University of Tennessee			
	Practice organ	2m	3s	3r
Cleveland, Ohio	First English Lutheran Church	2m	3s	3r
DeKalb, Illinois	Northern Illinois University	2m	9s	10r
Cincinnati, Ohio	Univ. of Cincinnati (Portatief)	1m	1s	1r
Minneapolis, Minn.	House organ (Regaal Portatief)	1m	1s	1r

1970

Sacramento, California	Westminster Presbyterian Church			
	Positief	1m	4s	5r
St. Petersburg, Fla.	Presbyterian College Chapel	2m	34s	45r
St. Petersburg, Fla.	House organ	2m	9s	10r
Rosemount, Minn.	Church of St. Joseph	1m	2s	2r

1971

Bristol, Virginia	Virginia Intermont College	2m	26s	34r
Oberlin, Ohio	House organ	2m	3s	3r
Weston, Connecticut	Emmanuel Church	2m	9s	10r
Atlanta, Georgia	House organ	2m	9s	10r
Cleveland, Ohio	House organ	2m	3s	3r
Winston-Salem, N. C.	Salem College, Practice organ	2m	3s	3r

1971

Portland, Oregon	Oregon Episcopal School			
	St. Helen's Hall	2m	11s	14r
Berkeley, Cal.	St. Mark's Church	2m	15s	19r
Santa Barbara, Cal.	University of California	2m	15s	18r
Wallingford, Conn.	The Choate School			
	Rosemary Hall	2m	15s	18r
Winston-Salem, N. C.	House organ	2m	13s	15r

1973
Fresno, California	St. James's Church (4' Positief)	1m	6s	10r
Sonora, California	St. James's Cathedral			
	2' Positief	1m	4s	5r
Minneapolis, Minn.	House organ (Portatief)	1m	2s	2r
New York, New York	House organ (4' Positief)	1m	3s	3r

1974
| Oberlin, Ohio | Oberlin Conservatory | 3m | 44s | 71r |

1975
Durham, N. C.	Duke University			
	Practice organ	2m	15s	18r
	Practice organ	2m	9s	10r
Concord, N. C.	First Presbyterian Church	3m	31s	39r

1976
Cleveland, Ohio	Trinity Cathedral	2m	13s	16r
Chico, California	California State University	1m	9s	11r
Pleasantville, N. Y.	St. John's Church	2m	9s	12r
Princeton, New Jersey	Westminster Choir College			
	Two practice organs	2m	4s	4r
Claremont, California	Pomona College	2m	9s	10r
Durham, N. C.	Duke University Chapel	4m	66s	102r
Swannanoa, N. C.	Warren Wilson College	2m	9s	9r

1977 (until September)
Summit, New Jersey	Unitarian Church	2m	12s	15r
Cleveland, Ohio	Trinity Cathedral	3m	39s	49r
Youngstown, Ohio	Youngstown State University	2m	9s	10r
Purchase, New York	State University of New York			
	(Originally built for Carnegie			
	Hall but never installed)	3m	43s	60r
Westfield, New Jersey	St. Paul's Church	2m	7s	7r

Completed after January 1, 1978
Youngstown, Ohio	Youngstown State University	2m	15s	18r
Durham, N. C.	St. Stephen's Church	3m	34s	46r
Bryn Mawr, Pa.	House organ	2m	7s	7r

APPENDIX B:
LIST OF DISPOSITIONS

1. Old Chapel, Salem College, Winston-Salem, North Carolina: 1957.
2. Busch-Reisinger Museum, Harvard University: 1958.
3. St. Andrew's Church, Montevallo, Alabama: 1958.
4. Reynolda Presbyterian Church, Winston-Salem, North Carolina: 1961.
5. St. Mark's Cathedral, Seattle, Washington: 1965.
6. Shirley Recital Hall, Salem College: 1965.
7. St. Anne's Church, Atlanta, Georgia: 1966.
8. All Saints' Church, Palo Alto, California: 1967.
9. First Congregational Church, Branford, Connecticut: 1969.
10. Virginia Intermont College, Bristol, Virginia: 1971.
11. St. Mark's Church, Berkeley, California: 1972.
12. Warner Hall, Oberlin Conservatory, Oberlin, Ohio: 1974.
13. First Presbyterian Church, Concord, North Carolina: 1975.
14. Warren Wilson College, Swannanoa, North Carolina: 1976.
15. Duke University Chapel, Durham, North Carolina: 1976.

DISPOSITIONS OF SELECTED INSTRUMENTS

Old Chapel, Salem College, Winston-Salem, North Carolina: 1957

HOOFDWERK		RUGWERK		PEDAAL	
Gedekt	8	Gedekt	8	Bourdon	16
Prestant	4	Roerfluit	4	Gedekt	8
Fluit	4	Prestant	2	Woudfluit	4
Octaaf	2	Quint	1⅓	Ruispijp	III
Mixtuur	III	Cimbel	I-II		
Sesquialter	II	Kromhoorn	8		

Busch-Reisinger Museum, Harvard University, Cambridge, Massachusetts: 1958

HOOFDWERK		RUGWERK		BORSTWERK		PEDAAL	
Prestant	8	Holpijp	8	Zingend gedekt	8	Bourdon	16
Roerfluit	8	Prestant	4	Koppelfluit	4	Prestant	8
Octaaf	4	Roerfluit	4	Prestant	2	Gedekt	8
Speelfluit	4	Gemshoorn	2	Sifflet	1	Fluit	4
Nasard	2⅔	Quint	1⅓	Regaal	8	Mixtuur	III
Vlakfluit	2	Mixtuur	II			Fagot	16
Terts	1⅗	Kromhoorn	8			Trompet	8
Mixtuur	IV						

St. Andrew's Church, Montevallo, Alabama: 1958

MANUAAL		PEDAAL
Holpijp	8	permanently coupled
Quintadeen	8	to manual
Prestant	4	
Roerfluit	4	
Gemshoorn	2	
Cymbel	II	

Reynolda Presbyterian Church, Winston-Salem, North Carolina: 1960

HOOFDWERK		POSITIEF		BORSTWERK		PEDAAL	
Quintadeen	16	Gedekt	8	Dulciana	8	Subbas	16
Prestant	8	Prestant	4	Lieflijk gedekt	8	Prestant	8
Roerfluit	8	Roergedekt	4	Spitsfluit	4	Bourdon	8
Octaaf	4	Gemshoorn	2	Prestant	2	Quint	5⅓
Nachthoorn	4	Sesquialter	II	Basson-Hobo	8	Fagot	16
Mixtuur	IV	Scherp	III	Quint	1⅓	Octaaf	4
Trompet	8	Kromhoorn	8			Trompet	4
						Mixtuur	IV

St. Mark's Cathedral, Seattle, Washington: 1965

HOOFDWERK		RUGWERK		BOVENWERK		BORSTWERK	
Prestant	16	Prestant	8	Prestant	8	Gedekt	8
Prestant	8	Gedekt	8	Fluit	8	Prestant	4
Roerfluit	8	Quintadeen	8	Gemshoorn	8	Fluit	4
Octaaf	4	Octaaf	4	Zweving	8	Nachthoorn	2
Speelfluit	4	Roerfluit	4	Octaaf	4	Larigot	1 ⅓
Quint	2 ⅔	Octaaf	2	Koppelfluit	4	Cymberl	I-II
Octaaf	2	Mixtuur	III	Nasard	2 ⅔	Regaal	8
Terts	1 ⅗	Scherp	III	Flageolet	2		
Mixtuur	IV	Sesquialter	II	Octaaf	1		
Scherp	III	Dulciaan	16	Plein Jeu	IV		
Trompet	16	Schalmei	8	Trompet	8		
Trompet	8			Kromhoorn	8		

PEDAAL	
Prestant	32
Prestant	16
Subbas	16
Octaaf	8
Gedekt	8
Octaaf	4
Spitsgedekt	4
Nachthoorn	2 + 1
Mixtuur	VII
Bazuin	16
Trompet	8
Trompet	4
Cornet	2

Shirley Recital Hall, Salem College: 1965

HOOFDWERK		BOVENWERK		BORSTWERK		PEDAAL	
Prestant	8	Gedekt	8	Gedekt	8	Quintadeen	16
Roerfluit	8	Prestant	4	Koppelfluit	4	Prestant	8
Octaaf	4	Fluit	4	Prestant	2	Bourdon	8
Fluit	4	Gemshoorn	2	Flageolet	1	Octaaf	4
Octaaf	2	Ruisquint	II	Regaal	8	Mixtuur	III
Mixtuur	III	Sesquialter	II			Fagot	16
Cornet	IV					Schalmei	4
Trompet	8						

St. Anne's Church, Atlanta, Georgia: 1966

HOOFDWERK		BORSTWERK		PEDAAL	
Quintadeen	16	Gedekt	8	Prestant	16
Prestant	8	Prestant	4	Bourdon	16
Roerfluit	8	Roerfluit	4	Octaaf	8
Spitsgamba	8	Woudfluit	2	Gedekt	8
Octaaf	4	Quint	1 ⅓	Spitsfluit	4
Speelfluit	4	Sexquialter	II	Mixtuur	III
Octaaf	2	Mixtuur	III	Fagot	16
Mixtuur	IV	Dulciaan	16	Schalmei	4
Trompet	8				

All Saints' Church, Palo Alto, California: 1969

N. B. There are two separate instruments in this church. Plate 3 shows the Hoofdorgel to the right and the smaller Positief to the left.

HOOFDWERK		BORSTWERK		PEDAAL	
Prestant	8	Gedekt	8	Subbas	16
Roerfluit	8	Roerfluit	4	Bourdon	8
Octaaf	4	Prestant	2	Octaaf	4
Fluit	4	Cymbel	I-II	Fluit	2
Octaaf	2	Sesquialter	II	Dulciaan	16
Mixtuur	IV	Regaal	8		
Trompet	8				
Cimbelster					

POSITIEF	
Holpijp	8
Prestant	4
Roerfluit	4
Gemshoorn	2
Quint (treble)	2⅔
Terts (treble)	1⅗
Mixtuur	II

First Congregational Church, Branford, Connecticut: 1969

HOOFDWERK		RUGWERK		PEDAAL	
Bourdon	16	Holpijp	8	Subbas	16
Prestant	8	Quintadeeen	8	Prestant	8
Roerfluit	8	Prestant	4	Gedekt	8
Voce Umana	8	Roerfluit	4	Octaaf	4
Octaaf	4	Gemshoorn	2	Fluit	2
Gedektfluit	4	Quintfluit	1⅓	Mixtuur	IV
Quintfluit	2⅔	Sifflet	1	Bazuin	16
Octaaf	2	Sesquialter	II	Trompet	8
Terts	1⅗	Scherp	IV	Clairon	4
Mixtuur	V	Dulciaan	16		
Cymbel	II	Cromorne	8		
Trompet	8	Cimbelster			
Trompet	4				

Virginia Intermont College, Bristol, Virginia; 1971

HOOFDWERK		BORSTWERK		PEDAAL	
Prestant	16	Gedekt	8	Subbas	16
Prestant	8	Quintadeen	4	Octaaf	8
Roerfluit	8	Roerfluit	4	Bourdon	8
Octaaf	4	Prestant	2	Octaaf	4
Gemshoorn	4	Quint	1 ⅓	Fluit	4
Nasard	2 ⅔	Scherp	III-IV	Nachthoorn	2
Fluit	2	Dulciaanregaal	8	Fagot	16
Terts	1⅗			Schalmei	4
Mixtuur	IV-VI				
Trompet	8				

St. Mark's Church, Berkeley, California: 1971

HOOFDWERK		BORSTWERK		PEDAAL	
Prestant	8	Gedekt	8	Subbas	16
Roerfluit	8	Koppelfluit	4	Bourdon	8
Octaaf	4	Gemshoorn	2	Quintadeen	4
Speelfluit	4	Flageolet	1		
Octaaf	2	Sesquialter	II		
Mixtuur	IV				
Dulciaan	8				

Warner Hall, Oberlin Conservatory, Oberlin, Ohio: 1974

HOOFDWERK		RUGWERK		BOVENWERK		PEDAAL	
Prestant	16	Prestant	8	Bourdon	16	Prestant	16
Octaaf	8	Quintadeen	8	Prestant	8	Subbas	16
Roerfluit	8	Gedekt	8	Holpijp	8	Octaaf	8
Octaaf	4	Octaaf	4	Octaaf	4	Octaaf	4
Quint	2 ⅔	Roerfluit	4	Spitsfluit	4	Nachthoorn	2
Octaaf	2	Octaaf	2	Nasard	2 ⅔	Mixtuur	VI
Mixtuur	V-VI	Nasard	1 ⅓	Fluit	2	Bazuin	16
Scherp	IV	Sesquialter	II	Terts	1⅗	Trompet	8
Cornet (treble)	V	Mixtuur	IV-V	Mixtuur	V	Trompet	4
Trompet	16	Kromhoorn	8	Tertscymbel	III	Cornet	2
Trompet	8			Schalmei	8		
Vox Humana	8			Dulciaan	8		

First Presbyterian Church, Concord, North Carolina: 1975

HOOFDWERK		RUGWERK		BOVENWERK		PEDAAL	
Prestant	8	Gedekt	8	Prestant	8	Subbas	16
Roerfluit	8	Quintadeen	8	Bourdon	8	Prestant	8
Octaaf	4	Prestant	4	Octaaf	4	Bourdon	8
Fluit	4	Roerfluit	4	Fluit	4	Fluit	4
Quint	2 ⅔	Octaaf	2	Nasard	2 ⅔	Fagot	16
Octaaf	2	Quint	1 ⅓	Woudfluit	2		
Mixtuur	IV	Sesquialter	II	Terts	1⅗		
Trompet	8	Scherp	III	Mixtuur	III		
		Kromhoorn	8	Schalmei	8		

Warren Wilson College, Swannanoa, North Carolina: 1975

MANUAAL I		MANUAAL II		PEDAAL	
Gedekt "A"	8	Gedekt "A"	8	Gedekt "B"	8
Prestant	4	Fluit	4	Quintadeen	4
Octaaf	2	Larigot	1⅓		
		Terts (from g)	1⅗		

Gedekt "A" is common to both manuals; Gedekt "B" is an independent rank of pipes.

Duke Chapel, Duke University, Durham, North Carolina: 1976

HOOFDWERK		RUGWERK		BOVENWERK		ECHO	
Prestant	16	Prestant	8	Prestant	8	Gedekt	8
Bourdon	16	Gedekt	8	Baarpijp	8	Principaal	4
Octaaf	8	Octaaf	4	Gedekt	8	Fluit	4
Roerfluit	8	Fluit	4	Quintadeen	8	Nachthoorn	2
Octaaf	4	Nasard	2⅔	Octaaf	4	Cornet	III
Quint	2⅔	Octaaf	2	Fluit	4	Hautbois	8
Octaaf	2	Fluit	2	Nasard	2⅔		
Terts	1⅗	Terts	1⅗	Fluit	2		
Mixtuur	V-VII	Larigot	1⅓	Terts	1⅗		
Scherp	IV-V	Sesquialter	II	Sifflet	1		
Cornet (treble)	V	Mixtuur	V-VI	Mixtuur	V-VI		
Bombarde	16	Scherp	IV-V	Trompet	8		
Trompet	8	Schalmei	8	Hautbois	8		
Trompette	8	Cromorne	8	Vox Humana	8		
Clairon	4	Trompet	4				
Trompeta Magna 16 (treble)							
Clarin (treble)	8	*en chamade*					
Trompeta Batalla (bass)	4						

PEDAAL			
Prestant	16		
Subbas	16	Rossignol	
Quint	10⅔	Cimbelster	
Octaaf	8		
Quint	5⅓		
Octaaf	4		
Nachthoorn	2		
Mixtuur	V-VI		
Bazuin	16		
Trompet	8		
Trompette	8		
Clairon	4		
Cornet	2		

APPENDIX C:
A SELECTIVE DISCOGRAPHY

The following is a summary of recordings of Flentrop organs in the United States and of Flentrop instruments and restorations in Europe, recorded for American firms.

Location	Cat. No.	Title or Repertoire
		Recordings for Columbia Records by E. Power Biggs.
Kruiskerk, Amstelveen	KSL 219	"Art of the Organ"
Michaelskerk, Zwolle	KL 5262	"Bach at Zwolle"
Busch-Reisinger Museum, Harvard	DL 5288	"The Organ" [Six-stop positief, not the 1957 three-manual instrument.]
	ML 5443, MS 6117	Gabrieli, Frescobaldi
	ML 5567, MS 6167	D'Aquin: *Noels*
	ML 5608, MS 6208	Soler: Six concerti for two organs.
	ML 5634, MS 6234	Hindemith: *Three Sonatas*
	ML 5661, MS 6261, MQ 435	*Bach Organ Favorites*
	ML 5737 MS 6337	Sweelinck: *Variations on Popular Songs*
	ML 5754, MS 6354, MQ 486	*Heroic Music for Organ, Brass and Percussion"*
	ML 6148, MS 6748, MQ 740, 16 11 0218	*Bach Organ Favorites, Vol. II*

	MS 7108, MQ 990	*Bach Organ Favorites, Vol. III*
	EPB-1	A Biggs Festival
	MS 7174,	Soler: Six concerti for two organs (re-issue)
	MGP 13	
		Our Best To You (including re-issue of Bach: "Toccata and Fugue in d-minor"
	MS 7424	*Bach Organ Favorites, Vol. IV*
	M 30539 MA 30539 MT 30539	*The Biggs Bach Book.*
	M 31424 MT 31424 MQ 31424 MA 31424 MAQ 31424	*Bach Organ Favorites, Vol. V*
	M 32735	D'Aquin: *Noëls* (re-issue)
	M 32791 MA 32791 MT 32791 MQ 32791 MAQ 32791	*Bach Organ Favorites, Vol. VI*
	D3M 33724	*Bach Organ Favorites* (re-issue)
	M4X 35180	*A Tribute to E. Power Biggs*
Michaelskerk, Zwolle Laurenskerk, Alkmaar	M2L 297, M2S 697	*The Golden Age of the Organ*
32 organs	KS 7263	*The Organ in Sight and Sound*
Laurenskerk, Alkmaar; Breda, Church of the Holy Sacrament	M 31961	*Famous Organs of Holland and North Germany*

Recordings released by other firms.

St. Mark's Cathedral Seattle	Cambridge 2515	Buxtehude, Lawrence Moe, organist

| Michaelskerk, Zwolle | Cambridge 2510 | *Elizabethan Organ Music,* Gustav Leonhardt, organist |
| Laurenskerk, Alkmaar | Cambridge 3508 | Sweelinck, Gustav Leonhardt, organist |

DIRK ANDRIES FLENTROP
Personal Chronology
(from *Flentrop Orgelbouw 75 Years*)

1910   Born 1 May.

1927-1930   Apprenticeship at Paul Faust, Schwelm, Germany
and at Frobenius & Co., Kgs. Lyngby, Denmark.

1928-1951   Organist, Reformed Church in Westzaan.

1940   Took over direction of firm from H. W. Flentrop.

1945   President, Protestant Organ Builders in the Netherlands.

1951   Establishment of workshop in Koog aan de Zaan.

1957-1965   Co-founder, International Society of Organ Builders and
President during that period; member of Executive Board
until 1978.

1968   Established workshop in Wapenveld.

1968   Honorary Doctorate, Oberlin College, Oberlin, Ohio.

1971   Established workshop in Odijk.

1976   Honorary Doctorate, Duke University, Durham, N. C.

1976   Made Officer of the Order of Oranje Nassau.

1976   Resigned as president and became President of Board of
Directors of Flentrop Orgelbouw.

1978   Resigned 1 January as President of the Board and turned
ownership of Flentrop Orgelbouw over to the Administration
and co-workers.

1978   Honorary membership, American Institute of Organ Builders.

SOURCES CITED IN THE TEXT

(When only the title of a work is given in a footnote, full information is to be found in this list.)

Adlung, Jacob. *Musica mechanica organoedi* (1723-27). Berlin, 1768. Facsimile, Kassel, 1931. Bärenreiter.

Bédos de Celles. *L'Art du Facteur d'Orgues,* Paris, 1766. Facsimile, Kassel, 1934. Bärenreiter. English translation and facsimile illustrations, Raleigh, 1977. Sunbury Press.

Biggs, E. Power. "The Classic Organ in the Germanic Museum." Tape made for the Smithsonian Institution, January 1973.

Biggs, Margaret P. Biography of E. Power Biggs in *A Tribute to E. Power Biggs,* Columbia Records, MAX 35180. See also discography in same booklet.

Correspondence: E. Power Biggs and D. A. Flentrop from 1955 on, concerning Busch-Reisinger Museum organ. C. B. Fisk and D. A. Flentrop, concerning collaboration between them and related subjects, from 1955. Fenner Douglass and D. A. Flentrop.

Diocese of Olympia, Seattle, Washington, 1962. *The Great Gift of Music.*

Douglass, F., Ferguson, J. G., and Flentrop, D. A. "The Benjamin N. Duke Memorial." Durham: Duke University, 1976.

Estada, Jesús. *Música y Músicos de la Epoca Virreinal.* México: S. E. P., 197?.

Ferguson, John Allen. *Walter Holtkamp, American Organ Builder.* Kent, Ohio, 1979. Kent State University Press.

Fesperman, J. *Organs in Mexico.* Raleigh, 1979. Sunbury Press.

Fesperman, J. *Two Essays on Organ Design.* Raleigh, 1975. Sunbury Press.

Fisk, Charles. "The Organ's Breath of Life." *Diapason,* September, 1973.

Flentrop, D. A. "Lecture for A. G. O. Convention, New York, 1956." Electrostatic copy from D. A. Flentrop.

Flentrop, D. A. *List of organs in the U. S. A. built by Flentrop Orgelbouw B. V. Zaandam* [to September 1977] Electrostatic copy from D. A. Flentrop.

Flentrop, D. A. [Electrostatic copy of notes for meeting at Trinity Cathedral, Cleveland, November 19, 1974.

Flentrop, D. A. "The Schnitger Organ in the Grote Kerk at Zwolle," *Organ Institute Quarterly* (Andover, Massachusetts) Summer 1957.

Flentrop, D. A. MS: "The Organ Movement in Europe." Lecture for American Institute of Organbuilders, Fargo, North Dakota. October 1978.

Flentrop, D. A. MS: "Restoration of Historical Organs in the Netherlands." Lecture for International Society of Organbuilders, July 11, 1978, Amsterdam.

Flentrop, D. A. "Sleeplade en Rugpositief" [Slider chest and Rugpositief]. *Het Orgel,*
September and October 1934.

Flentrop, D. A., and Douglass, Fenner. "Thoughts on organ design in the Netherlands." *Organ Institute Quarterly,* Vol. 5:2, Spring 1955. pp. 24-33.

Flentrop, D. A. "Three Lectures on Organbuilding." MS. in the Smithsonian Institution of lectures delivered at the Smithsonian on April 24 and 25, 1980.

Freeman and Rowntree. *Father Smith.* Oxford, 1977. Positif Press.
Grove's Dictionary of Music and Musicians, 6th Edition. "Flentrop Orgelbouw."

Hess, Joachim. *Disposition der Merkwaardigste Kerk-orgelen.* Gouda, 1774. Reprint, *ed.* Lam-
bert Erné, Utrecht, 1945. J. A. H. Wagenaar.

Howes, A. [?] "A Census: "American Modern Tracker Organs." *Organ Institute Quarterly,* 9:1, 1964.

Jongepier, Jan. 75 *Jaar Flentrop Orgelbouw,* [Drawings by Simon Schaper; based on conver-
sations with D. A. Flentrop and Hans Steketee.] Zaandam, 1978. Flentrop Orgelbouw.
English translation edition Zaandam, 1980. Flentrop Orgelbouw, distributed in
United States by Sunbury Press.

Klotz, Hans. *Über die Orgelkunst.* Kassel, 1934. Bärenreiter.

Mahrenholz, Christhard. *Die Orgelregister.* Kassel, 1930. Bärenreiter.

Mahrenholz, Christhard. *Die Berechnung des Orgelpfeifmensuren von Mittelalter bis zur Mitte
des neunzehten Jahrhunderts. Kassel,* 1938. Bärenreiter.

Pape, Uwe, ed. *The Tracker Organ Revival in America.* Berlin, 1978 [?] Pape Verlag. Publication
No. 65 of the *Gesellschaft der Orgelfreunde.*

Schweitzer, Albert. *Deutsche und Französische Orgelbaukunst und Orgelkunst.* Leipzig,
1927. Breitkopf und Härtel.

FOOTNOTES

1. He retained ownership of the firm and was *President Commissaris* (President of the Board of Directors) until January 1, 1978, being responsible for completion of the Duke Chapel organ and the restoration of the two organs in Mexico Cathedral. On that date, shares of the firm were transferred to Hans Steketee and most of the employees.

2. This total is taken from Flentrop's list "until September," 1977. See page 87. The *Organ Institute Quarterly*, XI:1, 1964, has "A Census: American Modern Tracker Organs" and Pape, *Tracker Organ Revival in America,* includes as Part 3 "Opus Lists of American and Canadian Organbuilders."

3. See, for instance, references to Walter Holtkamp (page 47) and to Charles Fisk (page 48).

4. Flentrop to Fenner Douglass, May 7, 1968.

5. Smit is probably the same Bernard ("Father") Smith who built many organs in England after 1666. See Freeman and Rowntree, *Father Smith,* p. 107.

6. "The Schnitger Organ in the Grote Kerk at Zwolle," p. 33.

7. *Vijfenzeventig Jaar Flentrop Orgelbouw,* pp. 36-38.

7a. "The Organ Movement in Europe."

8. *Vijfenzeventig Jaar Flentrop Orgelbouw,* p. 12.

9. *Het Orgel,* September & October 1934.

10. With Fenner Douglass, *Organ Institute Quarterly,* Vol. V:2, Spring, 1955.

11. Flentrop to Fesperman, November 7, 1979.

12. *Ibid,* September 24, 1979.

13. *Ibid.*

14. *Ibid.*

15. *Ibid,* March 18, 1978.

16. Douglass to Fesperman, January 27, 1979.

17. "The Organ Movement in Europe," October 1978.

18. Flentrop to Fesperman, July 20, 1979.

19. Willing to Fesperman, December 27, 1978.

20. *Vijfenzeventig Jaar Flentrop Orgelbouw,* p. 32.

21. All quotations in this chapter are from the Biggs-Flentrop correspondence from October 1956 onward.

22. Col. DL-5288 (1958) and Col. KS-7263 (1969).

23. See discography.

24. Flentrop to John Ferguson, as cited in *Walter Holtkamp, American Organ Builder,* p. 14.

25. Flentrop to Fesperman, September 24, 1979. For a full description of the Mount Calvary organ, see *Two Essays on Organ Design,* pp. 75-81.

26. Letters from E. Power Biggs to Peter Hallock, September 15 and October 1, 1961.

27. Dictated at Santpoort, June 1979.

28. For a fuller description of Holtkamp's prophetic experiments, see Ferguson, *Walter Holtkamp, American Organ Builder,* p. 36, *ff.*

29. "Behind the Pipes," *The Benjamin N. Duke Memorial,* p. 15.

30. Flentrop to Fesperman, September 24, 1979.

31. "Behind the Pipes," p. 17.

32. See Fisk, "The Organ's Breath of Life," *The Diapason,* September 1963.

33. *Vijfenzeventig Jaar Flentrop Orgelbouw,* p. 29.

34. "Organ Movement in Europe," October 1978.

35. Flentrop to Fesperman, September 24, 1979; references to Hans Steketee and Siem Doot, voicer.

36. "A Historical Perspective," *The Benjamin N. Duke Memorial,* pp. 8 & 15.

37. "Organ Movement in Europe," October 1978.

38. See *Organs in Mexico,* Chapter V, for Flentrop's fuller discussion of the Mexico Cathedral restorations.

39. *Ibid,* Quoted in full in Spanish and English in Appendix C. See also Estrada, *Musica y Musicos de la Epoca Virreinal.*

40. Flentrop to Fesperman, December 27, 1978.

INDEX